Mastering Dropshipping

A COMPREHENSIVE GUIDE TO BULIDING A SUCCESSFUL ONLINE STORE

TANVEER SIDHU

INDIA · SINGAPORE · MALAYSIA

ISBN 979-8-89446-665-1

Contents

Chapter 1

Introduction to Dropshipping

In the ever-evolving landscape of commerce, where digital technologies continue to reshape traditional business paradigms, dropshipping emerges as a compelling model that epitomizes the spirit of innovation and adaptability. As we embark on this journey into the world of dropshipping, let us first unravel the essence of this transformative business model, tracing its origins, evolution, and impact both globally and within the vibrant marketplace of India.

Unraveling Dropshipping: A Global Odyssey

At its core, dropshipping represents a departure from conventional retail practices, offering a streamlined approach to product distribution and sales. Unlike traditional retail models where merchants maintain physical inventory, often entailing significant upfront investments and logistical complexities, dropshipping operates on a fundamentally different premise. In the realm of dropshipping, entrepreneurs forge strategic partnerships with suppliers or wholesalers who handle the warehousing, inventory management, and shipment of products directly to customers upon purchase.

This unique arrangement bestows dropshipping a myriad of advantages, chief among them being the elimination of inventory management overheads and the mitigation of financial risks associated with unsold inventory. By leveraging the infrastructure of suppliers and wholesalers, dropshipping entrepreneurs can focus their resources and energies on core business activities such as marketing, customer service, and business development, thereby fostering agility, scalability, and profitability.

The global ascent of e-commerce giants like Amazon, eBay, and Shopify has catalyzed the proliferation of dropshipping businesses, democratizing access to entrepreneurial opportunities on a scale previously unimaginable. Through user-friendly platforms, robust logistics networks, and integrated payment gateways, these digital marketplaces empower individuals from diverse backgrounds and geographies to embark on their entrepreneurial journeys with minimal barriers to entry.

Dropshipping in the Indian Context: Navigating Opportunities and Challenges

In the context of India, a nation characterized by its cultural diversity, demographic dividend, and burgeoning digital economy, dropshipping assumes a unique significance. With a rapidly expanding middle class, increasing internet penetration, and a growing appetite for online shopping, India stands poised at the cusp of a retail revolution, with e-commerce emerging as a primary driver of economic growth and consumer empowerment.

Within this dynamic landscape, dropshipping emerges as a potent catalyst for entrepreneurship, offering a pathway for ambitious individuals to harness the vast potential of the Indian market without succumbing to the traditional barriers of entry associated with brick-and-mortar retail. However, navigating the intricacies of the Indian market requires a nuanced understanding of local preferences, regulatory frameworks, and logistical constraints.

While the promise of dropshipping in India is undeniable, it is not without its challenges. From navigating the complexities of taxation and import regulations to optimizing last-mile delivery logistics and managing customer expectations, dropshipping entrepreneurs must confront a myriad of hurdles on their path to success. Yet, it is precisely through strategic partnerships, innovative solutions, and unwavering determination that entrepreneurs can transcend these challenges and unlock the full potential of dropshipping in India.

Embarking on the Dropshipping Journey

As we embark on this exploration of dropshipping, traversing the realms of innovation, entrepreneurship, and commerce, we invite you to join us in unraveling the mysteries, seizing the opportunities, and confronting the challenges that define this captivating business model. Whether you're a seasoned entrepreneur seeking new avenues of growth or an aspiring business owner eager to chart your entrepreneurial course, the world of dropshipping beckons with boundless potential and transformative possibilities catalyzed.

Chapter 2

Finding Profitable Niches

In the labyrinth of e-commerce, where competition reigns supreme, and consumer preferences evolve at breakneck speed, the quest for a profitable niche stands as a cornerstone of dropshipping success. In this chapter, we embark on a journey into the heart of niche selection, unraveling the intricacies of identifying lucrative opportunities both in the vast expanse of global markets and within the diverse tapestry of India.

The Essence of Niche Selection

At its essence, the concept of a niche embodies specificity. Rather than casting a wide net in the hope of capturing a broad audience, successful dropshippers recognize the power of focus, honing in on narrow segments of the market where demand outstrips supply and competition remains manageable. By catering to the unique needs, preferences, and pain points of a distinct demographic or interest group, dropshippers can carve out a lucrative foothold in the fiercely competitive landscape of e-commerce.

Understanding the Importance of Profitable Niches

In the realm of dropshipping, where margins can be razor-thin, and advertising costs soar, the choice of niche assumes paramount importance. A profitable niche serves as the bedrock upon which successful dropshipping ventures are built, offering a fertile ground for sustainable growth, profitability, and long-term viability. By targeting niches characterized by passionate audiences, unmet needs, and untapped opportunities, dropshippers can position themselves as indispensable solutions providers, commanding premium prices and fostering customer loyalty in the process.

Exploring Global Trends and Insights

In the pursuit of profitable niches, savvy dropshippers cast their gaze beyond geographical boundaries, seeking inspiration from global trends, emerging industries, and cultural phenomena that transcend borders. From the explosive growth of sustainable and eco-friendly products to the burgeoning demand for niche hobbies and subcultures, the global marketplace offers a cornucopia of opportunities for enterprising entrepreneurs to explore and exploit.

By leveraging tools and resources such as Google Trends, social media analytics, and market research reports, dropshippers can gain invaluable insights into consumer behavior, identify emerging trends, and anticipate future demand patterns with precision and foresight. Armed with this knowledge, they can tailor their product offerings, marketing strategies, and brand messaging to resonate deeply with their target audience, driving engagement, conversion, and, ultimately, PR spirations waiting to be tapped by astute dropshippers.

To unearth profitable niches in the Indian market, dropshippers must immerse themselves in the rich tapestry of Indian culture, paying heed to regional nuances, linguistic diversity, and socio-economic dynamics that shape consumer behavior and purchasing patterns. Whether it's catering to the burgeoning demand for ethnic wear and traditional handicrafts or capitalizing on the wellness boom sweeping urban centers, the Indian market abounds with niche opportunities waiting to be discovered and exploited.

The Art and Science of Niche Validation

While the process of identifying potential niches may be exhilarating, it is the art and science of niche validation that ultimately separates successful dropshippers from the multitude of aspirants. Rather than relying on gut instincts or wishful thinking, astute entrepreneurs employ a systematic approach to validate the viability of potential niches, assessing factors such as market size, competition intensity, and profit potential with rigor and objectivity.

Through techniques such as keyword research, competitor analysis, and test marketing, dropshippers can gauge the feasibility of entering a particular niche with confidence and clarity. By soliciting feedback from target customers, conducting small-scale experiments, and iterating based on real-world data and insights, they can mitigate risks, refine their strategies, and position themselves for success in an ever-evolving marketplace.

Niche Hunting in the Global Market

Navigating the vast expanse of the global market requires a keen understanding of cross-cultural dynamics, regional preferences, and geopolitical trends that shape consumer behavior and market opportunities. From the bustling metropolises of North America to the burgeoning economies of Southeast Asia, the global marketplace teems with niches waiting to be discovered and capitalized upon by astute dropshippers.

To identify profitable niches in the global market, dropshippers must adopt a multifaceted approach that encompasses market research, trend analysis, and competitive intelligence. By studying emerging trends and consumer preferences across different regions and industries, dropshippers can unearth hidden gems and untapped opportunities that resonate with global audiences and transcend cultural boundaries.

Whether it's capitalizing on the rise of wellness and self-care products in Western markets or tapping into the growing demand for technology-driven solutions in emerging economies, the global marketplace offers a wealth of niche opportunities for enterprising entrepreneurs to explore and exploit. By embracing diversity, embracing innovation, and embracing the spirit of global entrepreneurship, dropshippers can position themselves for success in an interconnected world where borders are blurred, and possibilities abound.

Conclusion: The Power of Niche Proficiency

In the grand tapestry of dropshipping, where fortunes rise and fall with the tides of consumer sentiment and market dynamics, the choice of niche stands as a beacon of opportunity and resilience. By mastering the art of niche selection, entrepreneurs can transcend the constraints of commoditization and competition, forging deep connections with their audience and reaping the rewards of sustainable growth and profitability.

As you embark on your journey into the realm of niche proficiency, remember that success favors the bold, the curious, and the relentless. Embrace the spirit of exploration, experimentation, and adaptation, and let your quest for profitable niches be guided by a relentless pursuit of excellence and innovation. For in the world of dropshipping, as in life itself, the greatest rewards await those who dare to dream, to discover, and to deliver value beyond measure.

Chapter 3

Setting Up Your Online Store for Dropshipping

In the dynamic realm of e-commerce, where opportunities abound and innovation reigns supreme, the establishment of a robust online store serves as the cornerstone of dropshipping success. In this chapter, we embark on a journey into the intricacies of setting up an online store tailored specifically for dropshipping ventures. From choosing the right platform to optimizing user experience, we'll explore the essential steps and helpful websites to guide you on your path to e-commerce excellence.

The Foundation of Your Online Store

Before delving into the technical intricacies of building your online store, it's essential to lay a solid foundation grounded in clarity of purpose, target audience, and brand identity. Define your niche, identify your target market, and articulate your unique value proposition. Understanding your audience's needs, preferences, and pain points will inform every aspect of your online store, from product selection to website design and marketing strategy.

Choosing the Right Platform

When it comes to building your online store, the choice of platform plays a pivotal role in determining your store's functionality, scalability, and overall success. Fortunately, there's no shortage of options available, each catering to different needs, preferences, and budgets. Let's explore some of the most popular platforms and their features:

1. Shopify: Renowned for its user-friendly interface, robust features, and extensive app ecosystem, Shopify stands as a top choice for dropshippers seeking a hassle-free solution for building and managing their online store. With customizable themes, built-in marketing tools, and seamless integration with dropshipping apps like Oberlo, Shopify offers a comprehensive solution for entrepreneurs of all levels of experience.

2. WooCommerce: Built on top of WordPress, WooCommerce combines the flexibility of open-

source software with the power of the world's most popular content management system. With a vast array of plugins and themes, WooCommerce allows dropshippers to customize their online store to suit their specific needs and preferences, making it an ideal choice for those seeking complete control over their e-commerce operations.

3. BigCommerce: Positioned as a scalable solution for growing businesses, Big Commerce offers a feature-rich platform tailored to the needs of ambitious entrepreneurs. With built-in SEO tools, multi-channel selling capabilities, and enterprise-grade security features, BigCommerce empowers dropshippers to expand their reach, streamline their operations, and drive sustainable growth.

4. Magento: Ideal for larger businesses with complex requirements, Magento provides a robust platform that can handle high traffic volumes, extensive product catalogs, and advanced customization needs. While it may require more technical expertise to set up and manage, Magento offers unparalleled flexibility and scalability for dropshippers with ambitious growth plans.

Designing Your Online Store

Once you've chosen the right platform for your online store, it's time to focus on design. Your website's design plays a crucial role in shaping the user experience and influencing purchase decisions. Whether you opt for a pre-designed theme or invest in custom design services, prioritize simplicity, clarity, and ease of navigation. Ensure that your website is mobile-responsive, as an increasing number of consumers browse and shop on their smartphones and tablets.

Essential Elements of Your Online Store

As you build your online store, be sure to incorporate essential elements that enhance usability, trustworthiness, and conversion rates:

1. Clear Navigation: Make it easy for visitors to find what they're looking for by organizing your products into logical categories and using intuitive navigation menus.

2. High-Quality Imagery: Showcase your products with crisp, high-resolution images that highlight their features and benefits. Consider investing in professional product photography to elevate your brand image.

3. Compelling Product Descriptions: Craft persuasive product descriptions that captivate the imagination, convey value, and address common pain points. Use clear, concise language and include relevant details such as dimensions, materials, and care instructions.

4. Customer Reviews and Testimonials: Build trust and credibility by featuring customer reviews and testimonials prominently on your product pages. Encourage satisfied customers to leave feedback and showcase positive reviews to reassure hesitant buyers.

5. Secure Checkout Process: Prioritize security and privacy by implementing SSL encryption and offering multiple secure payment options. Streamline the checkout process to minimize friction and reduce cart abandonment rates.

Helpful Websites for Creating Your Online Store

In addition to e-commerce platforms, several websites offer valuable resources and tools to streamline the process of setting up and managing your online store:

1. Canva: Create eye-catching graphics, banners, and social media posts with Canva's intuitive design

tools. Whether you need a logo, product images, or promotional materials, Canva offers templates and customization options to suit your needs.

2. Unsplash: Access a vast library of high-quality, royalty-free images to enhance your website's visual appeal. From product photos to background images, Unsplash provides a wealth of resources to elevate your brand aesthetics.

3. Mailchimp: Build and manage your email marketing campaigns with Mailchimp's user-friendly platform. From automated welcome sequences to targeted promotional emails, Mailchimp helps you stay connected with your audience and drive sales.

4. Google Analytics: Gain valuable insights into your website's performance, visitor behavior, and conversion rates with Google Analytics. Track key metrics, identify areas for improvement, and make data-driven decisions to optimize your online store for success.

5. Zendesk: Provide exceptional customer support with Zendesk's comprehensive help desk software. Whether you need a live chat, email support, or ticket management, Zendesk helps you deliver timely, personalized assistance to your customers.

Conclusion: Building Your Online Empire

As you embark on the journey of setting up your online store for dropshipping, remember that success is not just about the destination but also the journey. Embrace the process of experimentation, iteration, and continuous improvement, and let your passion for your niche and dedication to your customers guide you every step of the way. With the right tools, resources, and mindset, you have the power to build a thriving e-commerce business that fulfills your entrepreneurial dreams and transforms the lives of your customers.

Chapter 4

Sourcing Products and Suppliers for Successful Dropshipping

In the intricate ecosystem of dropshipping, where success hinges upon the quality of products, reliability of suppliers, and efficiency of logistics, the process of sourcing products and forging strategic partnerships assumes paramount importance. In this chapter, we embark on a journey into the heart of product sourcing, exploring the nuances of finding reputable suppliers, selecting winning products, and navigating the intricacies of global and Indian markets.

Understanding the Role of Suppliers in Dropshipping

At the heart of every successful dropshipping venture lies a network of reliable suppliers who serve as the lifeblood of the operation. Suppliers play a pivotal role in sourcing high-quality products, managing inventory, and fulfilling orders with precision and efficiency. Building strong relationships with reputable suppliers is essential for ensuring product quality, timely delivery, and customer satisfaction, all of which are critical factors in the success of your dropshipping business.

Identifying Suppliers in India

In recent years, India has emerged as a vibrant hub for manufacturing and sourcing a diverse range of products, making it an attractive destination for dropshipping entrepreneurs seeking quality suppliers at competitive prices. From textiles and handicrafts to electronics and pharmaceuticals, India boasts a rich tapestry of industries and artisans ready to collaborate with ambitious entrepreneurs.

To identify suppliers in India, consider leveraging online marketplaces, trade directories, and industry associations that cater to specific niches. Websites such as India MART, Alibaba, and Trade India serve as valuable resources for connecting with suppliers across various industries and regions. Additionally, attending trade fairs, exhibitions, and networking events can provide opportunities to meet potential suppliers face-to-face and forge meaningful partnerships based on trust and mutual benefit.

Evaluating Suppliers in India

When evaluating suppliers in India, prioritize factors such as product quality, reliability, pricing, and communication. Conduct thorough due diligence by requesting samples, reviewing certifications and quality control processes, and soliciting references from other clients. Pay attention to the supplier's responsiveness, professionalism, and willingness to accommodate your specific needs and preferences.

In addition to assessing the supplier's capabilities, consider the logistical aspects of working with Indian suppliers, including shipping times, customs clearance procedures, and import regulations. Establish clear communication channels and expectations regarding order fulfillment, tracking, and customer service to ensure a smooth and seamless dropshipping experience for your customers.

Exploring Global Sourcing Opportunities

While India offers a wealth of sourcing opportunities for dropshipping entrepreneurs, the global marketplace presents a vast array of options for sourcing products that may not be available domestically or offer competitive advantages in terms of pricing, quality, or innovation. From China and Southeast Asia to Europe and North America, the world is teeming with manufacturers, wholesalers, and distributors eager to collaborate with ambitious dropshippers.

Sourcing Products from China

China stands as a global manufacturing powerhouse, producing a staggering array of products across virtually every industry imaginable. From electronics and apparel to home goods and consumer electronics, Chinese suppliers offer a diverse range of products at competitive prices, making them a popular choice for dropshippers worldwide.

To source products from China, consider leveraging online marketplaces such as Alibaba, AliExpress, and DHgate, which connect buyers with a vast network of suppliers and manufacturers. When evaluating Chinese suppliers, pay close attention to factors such as product quality, manufacturing capabilities, lead times, and communication. Request product samples, conduct factory inspections, and establish clear terms and expectations to mitigate risks and build trust with your Chinese suppliers.

Navigating Global Supply Chains

When sourcing products from global suppliers, it's essential to navigate the complexities of international supply chains, including shipping, customs, tariffs, and import regulations. Partnering with reputable freight forwarders, customs brokers, and logistics providers can help streamline the import process and ensure the timely delivery of your products to customers worldwide.

Additionally, cultural and language differences should be considered when communicating with overseas suppliers, and strong relationships should be built based on mutual respect, trust, and transparency. Invest in technology and tools that facilitate collaboration and streamline communication, such as video conferencing, project management software, and translation services.

Conclusion: Forging Strategic Partnerships for Success

As you embark on the journey of sourcing products and suppliers for your dropshipping business, remember that success is not just about finding the lowest prices or the highest-quality products. It's about building meaningful relationships with suppliers who share your values, understand your business goals, and are committed to helping you succeed.

Whether you're sourcing products from India, China, or elsewhere in the world, prioritize transparency, communication, and collaboration in your dealings with suppliers. Invest time and resources in building strong relationships based on trust, mutual respect, and shared objectives. By forging strategic partnerships with reputable suppliers, you can ensure a steady supply of high-quality products, minimize risks, and position your dropshipping business for long-term success in the fiercely competitive world of e-commerce.

Chapter 5

Product Research and Selection for Successful Dropshipping

In the fast-paced world of e-commerce, where trends come and go and consumer preferences evolve rapidly, the process of product research and selection stands as a linchpin of dropshipping success. In this chapter, we embark on a journey into the heart of product discovery, exploring strategies and techniques for identifying winning products, assessing market demand, and staying ahead of the competition in both Indian and global markets.

Understanding the Importance of Product Research

At the heart of every successful dropshipping venture lies a carefully curated selection of products that resonate with your target audience, address their needs, and inspire purchase decisions. Product research serves as the foundation upon which your entire dropshipping business is built, informing every aspect of your operations, from marketing and inventory management to customer service and beyond.

Identifying Profitable Niches

Before diving into product research, it's essential to first identify profitable niches within your target market. A niche represents a distinct segment of the market with specific needs, preferences, and characteristics that differentiate it from the broader market. By focusing on niche products, you can carve out a unique position in the market, minimize competition, and attract a loyal customer base.

To identify profitable niches, consider factors such as market size, competition intensity, and consumer demand. Leverage tools and resources such as Google Trends, keyword research tools, and social media analytics to uncover emerging trends, popular search queries, and niche opportunities within your target market. Additionally, conduct market research and competitor analysis to assess the viability and profitability of potential niches before committing resources to product sourcing and marketing.

Conducting Product Research

Once you've identified profitable niches, it's time to delve into product research to find winning products that meet the needs and preferences of your target audience. Product research involves evaluating a wide range of factors, including product demand, competition, pricing, and market trends, to identify products with the highest potential for success.

When conducting product research, consider the following strategies and techniques:

1. Keyword Research: Use keyword research tools such as Google Keyword Planner, SEMrush, and Ahrefs to identify popular search queries related to your niche and gauge the level of interest and demand for specific products. Look for keywords with high search volume and low-competition to uncover untapped opportunities for product sourcing and marketing.

2. Market Trends Analysis: Stay abreast of market trends and consumer preferences by monitoring industry publications, trade journals, and social media platforms. Identify emerging trends, fads, and viral products that have the potential to capture the attention of your target audience and drive sales.

3. Competitor Analysis: Analyze your competitors' product offerings, pricing strategies, and marketing tactics to identify gaps and opportunities in the market. Look for products with high demand and low-competition, as well as products that offer unique value propositions or solve specific pain points for consumers.

4. Supplier Research: Research potential suppliers and manufacturers to assess their product catalogs, pricing, quality standards, and reliability. Look for suppliers with a track record of delivering high-quality products on time and maintaining open lines of communication with their dropshipping partners.

5. Customer Feedback: Solicit feedback from your target audience through surveys, focus groups, and social media channels to understand their preferences, pain points, and purchase motivations. Use this feedback to inform your product selection process and identify products that resonate with your customers' needs and desires.

Selecting Winning Products

Armed with insights from your product research, it's time to select winning products that align with your niche, target audience, and business objectives. When selecting products for your dropshipping store, prioritize the following criteria:

1. Product Quality: Choose products that meet high standards of quality and craftsmanship to ensure customer satisfaction and minimize returns or complaints.

2. Market Demand: Select products with proven demand and a track record of sales success to maximize your chances of generating revenue and profitability.

3. Profit Margins: Evaluate the profitability of each product based on factors such as wholesale prices, shipping costs, and retail pricing. Choose products with healthy profit margins that allow you to cover expenses and generate a sustainable income.

4. Competitive Advantage: Look for products that offer a unique value proposition or differentiation compared to competitors. Consider factors such as product features, branding, packaging, and customer service to stand out in the crowded marketplace.

5. Scalability: Choose products that have the potential for scalability and long-term growth.

Avoid products with limited appeal or short-lived trends that may fizzle out quickly.

Conclusion: The Art and Science of Product Research

As you embark on the journey of product research and selection for your dropshipping business, remember that it's both an art and a science. Embrace the process of exploration, experimentation, and iteration, and let data and insights guide your decisions. Stay attuned to market trends, consumer preferences, and industry developments, and be prepared to adapt and evolve your product selection strategy over time.

By combining creativity, intuition, and analytical rigor, you can identify winning products that resonate with your target audience, drive sales, and propel your dropshipping business to new heights of success in both Indian and global markets.

Chapter 6

Creating Compelling Product Lists

In the vibrant world of e-commerce, where attention spans are fleeting, and competition is fierce, the art of creating compelling product lists stands as a linchpin of dropshipping success. In this chapter, we delve into the intricacies of crafting product listings that captivate, persuade, and convert browsers into buyers. From persuasive copywriting to stunning visuals, we'll explore the essential elements and best practices for creating product lists that stand out in the crowded marketplace.

Understanding the Power of Product Listings

A product listing serves as your digital storefront, providing potential customers with their first impression of your products and brand. A well-crafted product listing has the power to inform, inspire, and persuade consumers, guiding them through the purchase journey and instilling confidence in their buying decision. By investing time and effort into creating compelling product lists, you can differentiate your offerings, build trust with your audience, and drive sales in the fiercely competitive world of e-commerce.

Essential Elements of a Compelling Product List

When creating product lists for your dropshipping store, it's essential to include the following elements to maximize their effectiveness and appeal to your target audience:

1. High-Quality Product Images: Visuals are the first thing customers notice when browsing your product listings. Use high-resolution images that showcase your products from multiple angles and highlight key features. Invest in professional product photography or utilize supplier-provided images to ensure consistency and quality across your listings.

2. Persuasive Product Descriptions: Craft compelling product descriptions that entice readers, highlight

the benefits of your products, and address potential objections. Use persuasive language, storytelling techniques, and sensory imagery to evoke emotion and create a connection with your audience. Focus on communicating the value proposition of your products and how they can solve your customers' problems or enhance their lives.

3. Clear and Concise Titles: Your product titles should be clear, concise, and descriptive, conveying essential information about the product at a glance. Include relevant keywords and key selling points in your titles to improve search visibility and attract the attention of potential buyers. Avoid using generic or vague titles that fail to differentiate your products from competitors.

4. Detailed Product Specifications: Provide detailed information about your products, including dimensions, materials, colors, and other relevant specifications. Make it easy for customers to understand what they're purchasing and ensure transparency in your product listings. Consider including a size chart or measurement guide for apparel and other size-dependent products to help customers make informed purchasing decisions.

5. Social Proof and Reviews: Incorporate social proof elements such as customer reviews, ratings, and testimonials to build trust and credibility with your audience. Highlight positive feedback from satisfied customers and encourage users to leave reviews and share their experiences. Leverage user-generated content and social media integrations to showcase real-life examples of your products in action.

Optimizing Product Listings for Search and Conversion

In addition to creating compelling product lists, it's essential to optimize your listings for search engines and conversion. Follow these best practices to improve the visibility and effectiveness of your product listings:

1. Keyword Optimization: Conduct keyword research to identify relevant search terms and phrases related to your products. Incorporate these keywords strategically into your product titles, descriptions, and metadata to improve search rankings and attract organic traffic.

2. A/B Testing: Experiment with different elements of your product listings, such as images, titles, descriptions, and pricing, to identify what resonates

most with your audience. Use A/B testing and data analysis to refine your listings and optimize them for maximum conversion rates.

3. Mobile Optimization: Ensure that your product listings are optimized for mobile devices, as an increasing number of consumers browse and shop on smartphones and tablets. Use responsive design techniques, optimize page load times, and streamline the checkout process to provide a seamless mobile shopping experience.

4. Cross-Selling and Upselling: Use your product listings to suggest related or complementary products that customers may be interested in purchasing. Incorporate cross-selling and upselling techniques to increase average order value and encourage repeat purchases.

5. Call-to-Action (CTA): Include a clear and compelling call-to-action (CTA) in your product listings to prompt users to take the desired action, such as adding the item to their cart or completing the purchase. Use persuasive language and design elements to draw attention to your CTA and encourage engagement.

Chapter 7

Effective Marketing Strategies

In the dynamic world of dropshipping, where competition is fierce and consumer behavior is constantly evolving, effective marketing strategies are essential for attracting, engaging, and converting customers. In this chapter, we explore a variety of marketing tactics and strategies to help you stand out in the crowded marketplace, build brand awareness, and drive sales for your dropshipping business.

Understanding the Importance of Marketing

Marketing serves as the engine that drives growth and profitability in your dropshipping business. Whether you're a new entrant in the market or an established player looking to expand your reach, effective marketing strategies are essential for connecting with your target audience, communicating your value proposition, and persuading consumers to choose your products over the competition.

Setting Marketing Objectives

Before diving into the tactics and techniques of marketing, it's essential to establish clear objectives and goals for your marketing efforts. Whether your aim is to increase brand awareness, drive website traffic, boost sales, or improve customer retention, defining specific, measurable, and achievable objectives will guide your marketing strategy and ensure that your efforts are aligned with your business goals.

Developing a Comprehensive Marketing Plan

A comprehensive marketing plan outlines the strategies, tactics, and channels you'll use to reach your target audience and achieve your marketing objectives. Your marketing plan should encompass both online and offline channels, including digital marketing, social media, email marketing, content marketing, influencer partnerships, and more. By diversifying your marketing efforts across multiple channels, you can maximize your reach and effectiveness and engage consumers at various touchpoints throughout their purchase journey.

Digital Marketing Strategies

Digital marketing encompasses a wide range of tactics and techniques for reaching and engaging consumers online. Let's explore some of the most effective digital marketing strategies for dropshipping businesses:

1. Search Engine Optimization (SEO): Optimize your website and product listings for search engines to improve your visibility and rankings in organic search results. Conducted keyword research, optimized metadata, and created high-quality, relevant content to attract organic traffic and drive sales.

2. Search Engine Marketing (SEM): Supplement your organic search efforts with paid search advertising on platforms such as Google Ads and Bing Ads. Use targeted keywords, compelling ad copy, and strategic bidding strategies to reach users actively searching for products like yours and drive traffic to your website.

3. Social Media Marketing: Leverage the power of social media platforms such as Facebook, Instagram, Twitter, and LinkedIn to connect with your audience, build brand awareness, and drive engagement. Create compelling content, run targeted ad campaigns, and engage with your

followers to foster meaningful relationships and drive traffic to your website.

4. Email Marketing: Build and nurture relationships with your audience through email marketing campaigns. Segment your email list based on user behavior, preferences, and purchase history, and deliver personalized, relevant content and offers to drive engagement and conversions.

5. Content Marketing: Create valuable, informative content that educates, entertains, and inspires your audience. Publish blog posts, articles, videos, infographics, and other content formats that address common pain points, answer questions, and provide solutions related to your niche. Use content marketing to establish your brand as a trusted authority and attract organic traffic to your website.

Offline Marketing Strategies

While digital marketing often takes center stage in today's digital-first world, offline marketing strategies can still be effective for reaching and engaging local audiences and driving foot traffic to your brick-and-mortar store or pop-up shop. Let's explore some offline marketing strategies for dropshipping businesses:

1. Local Events and Sponsorships: Participate in local events, trade shows, and community festivals to showcase your products and connect with potential customers face-to-face. Consider sponsoring events or partnering with local organizations to increase brand visibility and support your community.

2. Direct Mail Marketing: Send targeted direct mail campaigns to local households or businesses to promote special offers, new product launches, or upcoming events. Use eye-catching designs, compelling copy, and personalized messaging to capture attention and drive engagement.

3. Networking and Referral Programs: Build relationships with local businesses, influencers, and community leaders to expand your network and reach new audiences. Offer referral incentives or affiliate programs to encourage satisfied customers and partners to refer others to your business.

4. Guerrilla Marketing: Get creative with guerrilla marketing tactics such as street art, chalk stencils, or flash mobs to grab attention and generate buzz around your brand. Use unconventional, attention-

grabbing tactics to make a memorable impression and stand out from the competition.

Measuring and Optimizing Marketing Performance

Once you've implemented your marketing strategies, it's essential to monitor and measure their performance to determine their effectiveness and identify areas for improvement. Use key performance indicators (KPIs) such as website traffic, conversion rates, customer acquisition cost (CAC), return on investment (ROI), and Customer Lifetime Value (CLV) to track the success of your marketing campaigns and make data-driven decisions.

Continuously test and optimize your marketing strategies by experimenting with different tactics, messaging, and targeting parameters. Use A/B testing, multivariate testing, and data analysis to identify what works best for your audience and refine your approach accordingly. By adopting a data-driven, iterative approach to marketing, you can maximize the impact of your efforts and drive sustainable growth for your dropshipping business.

Conclusion: Driving Success Through Effective Marketing

As you navigate the ever-changing landscape of dropshipping, remember that effective marketing is the key to unlocking growth, profitability, and long-term success. By developing a comprehensive marketing plan, leveraging digital and offline marketing strategies, and measuring and optimizing your performance, you can attract, engage, and convert customers at every stage of their purchase journey and build a thriving dropshipping business that stands the test of time.

Chapter 8

Building a Strong Brand

In the dynamic world of dropshipping, where competition is fierce and consumer expectations are higher than ever, building a strong brand is essential for success. A strong brand not only differentiates your business from competitors but also creates emotional connections with customers, fosters loyalty, and drives long-term growth. In this chapter, we explore the key elements and strategies for building a strong brand that resonates with your audience and sets your dropshipping business apart from the competition.

Understanding the Power of Branding

Branding is more than just a logo or a catchy slogan—it's the essence of your business, encompassing everything from your visual identity and messaging to your values and customer experience. A strong brand communicates who you are, what you stand for, and why customers should choose you over the competition. By investing in branding, you can build trust, credibility, and loyalty with your audience, creating a lasting impression that transcends individual products and transactions.

Defining Your Brand Identity

At the heart of every strong brand lies a clear and compelling brand identity that resonates with your target audience and sets you apart from competitors. Your brand identity encompasses several key elements, including:

1. Brand Values: Define the core values and principles that guide your business and shape your brand's identity. Consider what you stand for, what you believe in, and how you want to be perceived by your audience. Your brand values should align with the needs and preferences of your target market and reflect your commitment to delivering exceptional value and customer experience.

2. Brand Voice and Tone: Develop a distinct brand voice and tone that reflects your brand's personality and resonates with your audience. Whether you're playful and irreverent or serious and authoritative, consistency in tone and messaging is key to building

brand recognition and establishing rapport with customers.

3. Visual Identity: Create a cohesive visual identity that reflects your brand's personality and values. This includes elements such as your logo, color palette, typography, and imagery. Invest in professional graphic design and branding services to ensure that your visual identity is polished, memorable, and aligned with your brand's positioning and objectives.

4. Brand Story: Craft a compelling brand story that resonates with your audience and communicates the origins, values, and mission of your business. Share your journey, your passion, and your vision in a way that engages and inspires customers, forging emotional connections and building brand loyalty in the process.

Creating a Memorable Brand Experience

A strong brand is built not only through visual identity and messaging but also through the customer experience you deliver at every touchpoint. From the moment a customer discovers your brand to the post-purchase interaction, every interaction shapes their perception of your brand and influences their likelihood to return and recommend you to others. Here are some key elements of creating a memorable brand experience:

1. User-Friendly Website: Design a user-friendly website that reflects your brand's visual identity and provides a seamless, intuitive shopping experience. Optimize navigation, streamline the checkout process, and prioritize mobile responsiveness to ensure that customers can easily find what they're looking for and complete their purchase hassle-free.

2. Exceptional Customer Service: Invest in exceptional customer service to delight and exceed customer expectations at every opportunity. Be responsive, helpful, and empathetic in your interactions, and go above and beyond to resolve issues and address concerns promptly. A positive customer service experience can turn satisfied customers into loyal brand advocates who sing your praises to others.

3. Branded Packaging and Unboxing Experience: Pay attention to the details of your packaging and unboxing experience to create a memorable, shareable moment for customers. Use branded packaging materials, personalized notes, and special touches to surprise and delight customers

when they receive their orders, reinforcing your brand's identity and fostering a sense of connection and appreciation.

4. Consistent Branding Across Channels: Maintain consistency in your branding across all channels and touchpoints, including your website, social media profiles, email communications, and advertising campaigns. Use consistent messaging, imagery, and design elements to reinforce your brand identity and ensure a cohesive brand experience for customers wherever they encounter your brand.

Building Brand Awareness and Engagement

Once you've defined your brand identity and created a memorable brand experience, it's time to focus on building brand awareness and engagement to attract and retain customers. Here are some effective strategies for building brand awareness and engagement:

1. Content Marketing: Create valuable, informative content that educates, entertains, and inspires your audience. Publish blog posts, articles, videos, and infographics that address common pain

points, answer questions, and provide solutions related to your niche. Use content marketing to establish your brand as a trusted authority and attract organic traffic to your website.

2. Social Media Marketing: Leverage the power of social media platforms such as Facebook, Instagram, Twitter, and LinkedIn to connect with your audience, build brand awareness, and drive engagement. Create compelling content, run targeted ad campaigns, and engage with your followers to foster meaningful relationships and build a loyal community around your brand.

3. Influencer Partnerships: Collaborate with influencers and content creators in your niche to reach new audiences and amplify your brand's reach and visibility. Identify influencers whose values align with your brand and whose audience demographics match your target market, and work together on sponsored content, product reviews, and promotional campaigns to increase brand awareness and drive sales.

4. Email Marketing: Build and nurture relationships with your audience through email marketing campaigns. Segment your email list based on user behavior, preferences, and purchase history, and

deliver personalized, relevant content and offers to drive engagement and conversions. Use email marketing to stay at the top of your audience's mind and encourage repeat purchases and referrals.

5. Partnerships and Collaborations: Partner with other brands, organizations, or influencers in complementary niches to cross-promote each other's products and reach new audiences. Collaborate on co-branded campaigns, events, or product launches to leverage each other's strengths and expand your reach and influence in the market.

Measuring Brand Performance and Impact

As you implement your branding strategies and initiatives, it's essential to measure their performance and impact to determine their effectiveness and identify areas for improvement. Use key performance indicators (KPIs) such as brand awareness, brand sentiment, customer engagement, and customer loyalty to track the success of your branding efforts and make data-driven decisions.

Monitor brand mentions and sentiment on social media and review platforms to gauge customer perception and sentiment toward your brand. Conduct brand awareness surveys and customer satisfaction surveys to gather feedback from your audience and identify areas for improvement. Use web analytics tools, social media analytics, and email marketing metrics to track the reach, engagement, and conversion rates of your branding initiatives and campaigns.

Chapter 9

Managing Inventory and Fulfillment

In the intricate dance of dropshipping, where customer satisfaction hinges on timely delivery and product quality, mastering inventory management and fulfillment processes is paramount. In this chapter, we explore the intricacies of inventory management, order fulfillment, and logistics, offering insights and strategies to streamline operations, optimize efficiency, and delight customers at every step of their purchase journey.

Understanding Inventory Management in Dropshipping

Inventory management lies at the heart of every successful dropshipping operation, encompassing the processes and systems used to track, monitor, and control the flow of goods from suppliers to customers.

Effective inventory management ensures that you have the right products in stock at the right time, minimizes stockouts and overstock situations, and maximizes operational efficiency and profitability.

Key Components of Inventory Management

Inventory management involves several key components and processes, including:

1. Inventory Tracking: Implement systems and tools to track and monitor your inventory levels in real time. Whether you use a spreadsheet, inventory management software, or a custom-built solution, ensure that you have visibility into your stock levels, reorder points, and product performance metrics to make informed decisions and avoid stockouts or overstock situations.

2. Demand Forecasting: Use historical sales data, market trends, and customer insights to forecast demand for your products accurately. Anticipate seasonal fluctuations, promotional events, and other factors that may impact demand and adjust your inventory levels accordingly to ensure adequate stock availability and prevent excess inventory buildup.

3. Supplier Management: Maintain strong relationships with your suppliers and manufacturers to ensure reliable and timely fulfillment of orders. Communicate proactively with suppliers, monitor lead times, and address any issues or delays promptly to minimize disruptions to your supply chain and maintain high service levels for your customers.

4. Order Processing: Develop efficient order processing workflows to streamline the fulfillment process and minimize order processing times. Automate repetitive tasks, such as order entry and invoicing, and integrate your order management system with your e-commerce platform and other business systems to ensure seamless order processing and fulfillment.

Optimizing Order Fulfillment

Order fulfillment is the process of picking, packing, and shipping orders to customers in a timely and efficient manner. In dropshipping, where suppliers handle the fulfillment process on your behalf, optimizing order fulfillment involves coordinating with suppliers, managing customer expectations, and ensuring that orders are processed and delivered accurately and on time.

Effective Order Fulfillment Strategies

To optimize order fulfillment in dropshipping, consider the following strategies and best practices:

1. Automate Order Processing: Leverage automation tools and technologies to streamline order processing and fulfillment workflows. Integrate your e-commerce platform with your supplier's systems to automate order routing, inventory updates, and shipping notifications, reducing manual effort and minimizing errors.

2. Monitor Order Status and Tracking: Maintain visibility into the status of orders and shipments at every stage of the fulfillment process. Use order tracking tools and systems to monitor order progress, track shipments in transit, and proactively communicate with customers about their order status and expected delivery dates.

3. Implement Quality Control Measures: Establish quality control processes to ensure that orders are picked, packed, and shipped accurately and according to customer specifications. Conduct regular audits and inspections of incoming inventory and outgoing shipments to verify product quality, accuracy, and compliance with customer requirements.

4. Offer Expedited Shipping Options: Provide customers with expedited shipping options, such as express or overnight shipping, to meet their urgent delivery needs and enhance the customer experience. Partner with logistics providers that offer fast and reliable shipping services and negotiate competitive rates to minimize shipping costs and transit times.

5. Handle Returns and Exchanges Efficiently: Develop clear and transparent return and exchange policies to facilitate hassle-free returns and exchanges for customers. Provide easy-to-follow instructions for initiating returns, offer pre-paid return labels where possible, and process refunds or replacements promptly upon receipt of returned merchandise.

Managing Inventory Risks and Challenges

While effective inventory management and order fulfillment are essential for dropshipping success, they also come with their fair share of risks and challenges. Common inventory management challenges in dropshipping include:

1. Stockouts and Overstock: Balancing inventory levels to avoid stockouts while minimizing the

risk of overstock situations can be challenging, especially in volatile or seasonal markets.

2. Supplier Reliability: Dependence on suppliers for inventory fulfillment exposes dropshippers to the risk of supplier delays, stockouts, or quality issues that can impact customer satisfaction and retention.

3. Shipping Delays and Logistics Issues: External factors such as weather disruptions, transportation delays, and customs clearance issues can impact shipping times and lead to customer dissatisfaction.

4. Inventory Shrinkage and Loss: Losses due to theft, damage, or inaccuracies in inventory tracking can erode profitability and undermine the efficiency of inventory management processes.

Mitigating Inventory Risks and Challenges

To mitigate inventory risks and challenges in dropshipping, consider the following strategies and tactics:

1. Diversify Suppliers: Work with multiple suppliers and manufacturers to diversify your supply chain

and minimize the risk of disruptions due to supplier issues or inventory shortages.

2. Implement Safety Stock: Maintain safety stock or buffer inventory to guard against unexpected spikes in demand or supplier delays and ensure continuity of supply for critical products.

3. Monitor Key Performance Indicators: Track key performance indicators (KPIs) such as inventory turnover, fill rate, and order accuracy to identify trends, detect potential issues, and make data-driven decisions to optimize inventory management processes.

4. Invest in Technology: Leverage inventory management software, order management systems, and other technology solutions to automate and streamline inventory management and fulfillment workflows, improve accuracy, and reduce manual effort.

Chapter 10

Customer Service and Support

In the fast-paced and ever-evolving landscape of dropshipping, where customer expectations are higher than ever, delivering exceptional customer service and support is paramount. In this chapter, we delve into the importance of customer service, explore strategies for providing outstanding support to your customers, and discuss how to turn challenges into opportunities for building lasting relationships and driving business growth.

Understanding the Importance of Customer Service

Customer service is the backbone of any successful dropshipping business, serving as the primary point of contact between you and your customers. It encompasses the entire customer journey, from pre-purchase inquiries and order processing to post-purchase support and issue resolution. Exceptional customer service not only satisfies immediate needs but also builds trust, fosters loyalty, and creates advocates who spread positive word-of-mouth about your brand.

Key Components of Customer Service

Providing outstanding customer service involves several key components and principles:

1. Responsive Communication: Be responsive and accessible to your customers across multiple channels, including email, phone, live chat, and social media. Respond promptly to inquiries, address concerns, and provide timely updates on order status and issue resolution to keep customers informed and engaged.

2. Empathy and Understanding: Approach each customer interaction with empathy, understanding, and a willingness to listen. Put yourself in the customer's shoes, acknowledge their concerns, and demonstrate genuine care and concern for their needs and preferences.

3. Transparency and Honesty: Be transparent and honest in your communications with customers, especially when addressing issues or resolving

disputes. Admit mistakes, take responsibility for any errors or shortcomings, and communicate openly about steps taken to rectify the situation and prevent recurrence.

4. Proactive Support: Anticipate customer needs and proactively offer assistance and guidance throughout the customer journey. Provide product recommendations, answer questions, and offer personalized support to help customers make informed purchasing decisions and navigate any challenges they may encounter.

5. Continuous Improvement: Regularly solicit feedback from customers and use it to identify areas for improvement and refine your customer service processes and practices. Monitor customer satisfaction metrics, such as Net Promoter Score (NPS) and customer satisfaction (CSAT) ratings, and use them to track performance and measure the effectiveness of your customer service efforts.

Strategies for Providing Exceptional Customer Service

To provide exceptional customer service and support in dropshipping, consider implementing the following strategies and best practices:

1. Invest in Training and Development: Train your customer service team to deliver consistent, high-quality service that reflects your brand values and meets customer expectations. Provide ongoing training and professional development opportunities to enhance their skills, knowledge, and effectiveness in addressing customer needs and resolving issues.

2. Empower Your Team: Empower your customer service team to make decisions and take ownership of customer issues and inquiries. Give them the autonomy and authority to resolve issues quickly and efficiently without the need for constant oversight or approval.

3. Implement Multi-Channel Support: Offer customer support across multiple channels to accommodate diverse customer preferences and communication styles. Provide options such as email, phone, live chat, and social media support, and ensure that customers can easily reach you whenever they need assistance.

4. Utilize Help Desk Software: Invest in help desk software or customer relationship management (CRM) tools to streamline customer service workflows, centralize customer interactions,

and track issues and inquiries from initiation to resolution. Use automation and self-service options to improve efficiency and enhance the customer experience.

5. Personalize the Experience: Personalize the customer experience by addressing customers by name, referencing past interactions or purchases, and tailoring recommendations and solutions to their specific needs and preferences. Show customers that you value their business and appreciate their loyalty by going the extra mile to make their experience memorable and meaningful.

Turning Challenges into Opportunities

While providing exceptional customer service is essential for success in dropshipping, it also comes with its fair share of challenges and obstacles. Common challenges in customer service include:

1. Managing High Volume: Handling a high volume of customer inquiries and support requests can strain resources and overwhelm your team, leading to delays and inefficiencies in issue resolution.

2. Dealing with Difficult Customers: Interacting with difficult or irate customers can be challenging and emotionally taxing for customer service

representatives, requiring patience, empathy, and conflict resolution skills to de-escalate tensions and resolve issues satisfactorily.

3. Navigating Language and Cultural Barriers: Serving a diverse customer base across different regions and cultures can pose challenges in communication and understanding, requiring sensitivity, cultural awareness, and language proficiency to bridge gaps and ensure effective communication and support.

4. Managing Returns and Refunds: Processing returns and refunds can be time-consuming and resource-intensive, especially in cases of product defects, shipping errors, or customer dissatisfaction. Balancing the need for customer satisfaction with the need to protect profitability and mitigate losses requires careful management and decision-making.

Chapter 11

Optimizing Your Website for Sales

In the fast-paced world of dropshipping, where competition is fierce, and consumer expectations are higher than ever, optimizing your website for sales is essential for success. In this chapter, we explore the strategies and techniques for creating a high-converting website that attracts visitors, engages customers, and drives sales.

Understanding the Importance of Website Optimization

Your website serves as the digital storefront for your dropshipping business, providing customers with their first impression of your brand and products. Optimizing your website for sales involves fine-tuning every element of your site—from design and navigation to content and functionality—to create a seamless, intuitive, and compelling user experience that inspires visitors to take action and make a purchase.

Key Components of Website Optimization

Optimizing your website for sales requires attention to detail and a strategic approach to design, content, and functionality. Key components of website optimization include:

1. Responsive Design: Ensure that your website is optimized for mobile devices, tablets, and desktops, with responsive design techniques that adapt to different screen sizes and resolutions. A mobile-friendly website is essential for providing a seamless browsing experience and maximizing conversions on mobile devices.

2. Clear Navigation: Streamline your website navigation to make it easy for visitors to find what they're looking for quickly and intuitively. Use clear menu structures, logical categorization, and prominent calls-to-action to guide users through your site and direct them to relevant products and content.

3. Compelling Visuals: Use high-quality images, videos, and graphics to showcase your products

and create a visually engaging experience for visitors. Invest in professional photography or utilize supplier-provided images to ensure that your product visuals are clear, captivating, and representative of your brand and offerings.

4. Persuasive Copywriting: Craft compelling product descriptions, headlines, and calls-to-action that communicate the value proposition of your products and compel visitors to take action. Use persuasive language, storytelling techniques, and sensory imagery to evoke emotion and create a connection with your audience.

5. Fast Load Times: Optimize your website load times to minimize page load times and ensure a smooth and seamless browsing experience for visitors. Compress images, minimize HTTP requests, and leverage caching and content delivery networks (CDNs) to improve site performance and reduce bounce rates.

6. Secure Checkout Process: Instill trust and confidence in your customers by ensuring that your checkout process is secure, streamlined, and user-friendly. Use SSL encryption, PCI compliance, and trusted payment gateways to protect customer data and facilitate seamless transactions.

Strategies for Website Optimization

To optimize your website for sales and maximize conversions, consider implementing the following strategies and best practices:

1. A/B Testing: Experiment with different elements of your website, such as headlines, images, calls-to-action, and product layouts, to identify what resonates most with your audience. Use A/B testing and multivariate testing to test variations and measure their impact on conversion rates and sales.

2. Conversion Rate Optimization (CRO): Focus on improving conversion rates by optimizing key elements of your website, such as product pages, checkout processes, and landing pages. Identify barriers to conversion, such as confusing navigation or slow load times, and implement changes to remove friction and facilitate conversions.

3. Search Engine Optimization (SEO): Optimize your website for search engines to improve visibility and attract organic traffic. Conduct keyword research, optimize metadata, and create high-quality, relevant content that aligns with user intent and addresses common search queries related to your products and niche.

4. Email Capture and Lead Generation: Capture email addresses and build your subscriber list by offering incentives such as discounts, freebies, or exclusive content. Use lead magnets, pop-up forms, and exit-intent overlays to encourage visitors to subscribe to your email list and stay engaged with your brand.

5. Personalization and Segmentation: Personalize the browsing experience for visitors by segmenting them based on their interests, preferences, and purchase history. Use data-driven insights to deliver relevant product recommendations, personalized offers, and targeted messaging that resonate with each segment of your audience.

6. Social Proof and Trust Signals: Incorporate social proof elements such as customer reviews, ratings, and testimonials to build trust and credibility with your audience. Showcase positive feedback from satisfied customers and highlight endorsements or endorsements from trusted sources to reassure visitors and alleviate concerns.

Measuring and Analyzing Performance

As you optimize your website for sales, it's essential to measure and analyze performance to track progress, identify opportunities for improvement, and make data-driven decisions. Key metrics to monitor include:

1. Conversion Rate: Measure the percentage of visitors who complete a desired action, such as making a purchase or signing up for your email list. Track conversion rates for different pages and elements of your website to identify areas for optimization and improvement.

2. Average Order Value (AOV): Monitor the average order value of transactions on your website to assess the effectiveness of cross-selling and upselling strategies. Identify opportunities to increase AOV by offering bundled products, volume discounts, or complementary items at checkout.

Chapter 12

Scaling Your Dropshipping Business

Scaling your dropshipping business is the process of expanding your operations, increasing your sales volume, and growing your revenue while maintaining efficiency and profitability. In this chapter, we'll delve into the strategies and best practices for scaling your dropshipping business effectively and sustainably.

Understanding the Challenges of Scaling

Scaling a dropshipping business comes with its unique set of challenges and considerations. These may include:

1. Logistical Complexities: As your business grows, managing inventory, order fulfillment, and logistics become more complex. Ensuring timely delivery, minimizing shipping costs, and maintaining

inventory accuracy become critical factors in maintaining customer satisfaction.

2. Supplier Relationships: Scaling may strain relationships with suppliers, especially if they're unable to keep up with increased demand or if quality issues arise. Maintaining open communication, negotiating favorable terms, and diversifying your supplier base can help mitigate these risks.

3. Operational Efficiency: Scaling requires optimizing and streamlining your operations to accommodate increased sales volume while minimizing costs and maximizing profitability. This may involve automating processes, investing in technology, and hiring additional staff to handle growing demand.

4. Customer Experience: Maintaining a high level of customer service and satisfaction becomes increasingly challenging as your customer base expands. Ensuring consistent quality, timely support, and personalized engagement becomes essential to retain customers and foster loyalty.

Strategies for Scaling Your Dropshipping Business

To scale your dropshipping business effectively and sustainably, consider implementing the following strategies:

1. Optimize Your Supply Chain: Streamline your supply chain to improve efficiency, reduce costs, and minimize lead times. Work closely with suppliers to optimize inventory management, forecast demand accurately, and ensure reliable fulfillment to meet customer expectations.

2. Invest in Technology: Leverage technology to automate and streamline key aspects of your business operations, such as order processing, inventory management, and customer support. Implementing an integrated e-commerce platform, inventory management system, and CRM software can help improve efficiency and scalability.

3. Expand Your Product Range: Diversify your product offerings to appeal to a broader audience and capture new market segments. Conduct market research to identify trending products, niche opportunities, and complementary product lines that align with your target market and business objectives.

4. Optimize Your Marketing Strategies: Refine your marketing strategies to reach a wider audience, increase brand awareness, and drive traffic to your website. Experiment with different marketing channels, such as social media, email marketing, influencer partnerships, and paid advertising, to identify what works best for your business.

5. Focus on Customer Retention: Prioritize customer retention efforts to maximize the lifetime value of your customers and foster long-term relationships. Implement loyalty programs, personalized marketing campaigns, and proactive customer support initiatives to keep customers engaged and satisfied.

6. Scale Your Team Thoughtfully: As your business grows, consider expanding your team to handle increased workload and responsibilities. Hire skilled professionals in key areas such as marketing, customer service, and operations to support your growth objectives and maintain service quality.

7. Monitor Key Performance Indicators (KPIs): Track and analyze key performance indicators (KPIs) to measure the success of your scaling efforts and identify areas for improvement. Monitor metrics such as sales growth, customer acquisition cost

(CAC), Customer Lifetime Value (CLV), and return on investment (ROI) to assess the effectiveness of your strategies and make data-driven decisions.

Mitigating Risks and Challenges

Scaling your dropshipping business involves inherent risks and challenges that must be addressed to ensure successful growth. Some common risks and challenges include:

1. Cash Flow Constraints: Rapid growth can strain cash flow due to increased inventory costs, marketing expenses, and operational overhead. Monitor your cash flow closely, plan for contingencies, and explore financing options such as business loans or lines of credit to support growth initiatives.

2. Quality Control Issues: As your business expands, maintaining consistent product quality and customer service becomes more challenging. Implement quality control measures, conduct regular audits, and monitor customer feedback to identify and address any issues promptly.

3. Market Saturation: In competitive markets, scaling too quickly can lead to market saturation and increased competition. Conduct thorough market research, identify niche opportunities,

and differentiate your brand through unique value propositions to stand out from competitors.

4. Operational Bottlenecks: Scaling can expose operational inefficiencies and bottlenecks that hinder growth and scalability. Continuously evaluate your processes, identify areas for improvement, and implement solutions to streamline operations and improve productivity.

Conclusion: Achieving Sustainable Growth

Scaling your dropshipping business is a complex and challenging endeavor that requires careful planning, strategic execution, and continuous optimization. By focusing on optimizing your supply chain, investing in technology, expanding your product range, and prioritizing customer retention, you can achieve sustainable growth and position your business for long-term success in the competitive e-commerce landscape.

Embrace scalability as a strategic imperative and approach growth with agility, adaptability, and a commitment to excellence. Continuously monitor market dynamics, customer preferences, and industry trends, and be prepared to pivot and evolve your strategies to capitalize on new opportunities and overcome challenges as they arise. With a strategic approach to scaling, you can unlock new levels of success and build a thriving dropshipping business that stands the test of time.

Chapter 13

Dealing with Returns and Refunds

Returns and refunds are inevitable in any e-commerce business, including dropshipping. While they can be challenging to manage, handling them effectively is crucial for maintaining customer satisfaction, fostering trust, and protecting your brand reputation. In this chapter, we'll explore the best practices, strategies, and considerations for managing returns and refunds in your dropshipping business.

Understanding the Importance of Returns and Refunds

Returns and refunds are an integral part of the customer experience in e-commerce, providing customers with peace of mind and assurance when making purchases online. By offering a hassle-free return and refund policy, you can instill confidence in your customers, encourage them to make purchases, and differentiate your brand from competitors.

Key Components of Returns and Refunds Policies

A well-defined returns and refunds policy is essential for setting expectations, protecting your business interests, and ensuring a smooth and transparent process for customers. Key components of a returns and refunds policy include:

1. Return Period: Specify the timeframe within which customers can initiate returns or request refunds, taking into account factors such as shipping times, product usage, and industry standards. Common return periods range from 30 to 60 days from the date of purchase.

2. Condition of Returned Items: Define the condition in which returned items must be in order to be eligible for a refund or exchange. Clearly communicate any requirements regarding original packaging, tags, and unused or unopened products to avoid disputes and misunderstandings.

3. Refund Methods: Outline the available refund methods, such as store credit, exchanges, or original payment refunds, and provide clear

instructions for initiating refunds. Specify any associated fees, processing times, or restrictions to manage customer expectations and prevent confusion.

4. Return Shipping: Clarify the responsibility for return shipping costs, including who bears the cost of return shipping and any applicable restocking fees or deductions from refunds. Consider offering pre-paid return labels or discounted shipping rates to simplify the return process for customers.

5. Exceptions and Restrictions: Identify any exceptions or restrictions to your returns and refund policy, such as final sale items, personalized or custom-made products, and hygiene-sensitive items. Clearly communicate these exceptions to customers to avoid misunderstandings and dissatisfaction.

Strategies for Managing Returns and Refunds

To effectively manage returns and refunds in your dropshipping business, consider implementing the following strategies and best practices:

1. Streamline the Returns Process: Simplify and automate the returns process to make

it as convenient and seamless as possible for customers. Provide clear instructions and easy-to-use online return portals or forms to facilitate returns and refunds and minimize the need for manual intervention.

2. **Provide Excellent Customer Support:** Offer responsive and empathetic customer support to assist customers with returns and refund inquiries and address any issues or concerns promptly. Ensure that customer service representatives are well-trained and equipped to handle return requests professionally and efficiently.

3. **Offer Flexible Return Options:** Provide customers with flexible return options, such as in-store returns, drop-off locations, or mail-in returns, to accommodate their preferences and convenience. Consider partnering with third-party logistics providers or local retailers to expand return options and reach a broader audience.

4. **Monitor Return Trends and Patterns:** Track and analyze return data to identify trends, patterns, and root causes of returns, such as product defects, sizing issues, or inaccurate product descriptions. Use this information to make data-driven decisions to improve product quality,

optimize product listings, and enhance the overall customer experience.

5. Implement Preventive Measures: Take proactive measures to prevent returns and minimize the likelihood of customer dissatisfaction. Provide detailed product descriptions, accurate sizing charts, and high-quality images to set clear expectations and reduce the risk of buyer's remorse or misunderstanding.

6. Manage Inventory and Stock Levels: Monitor inventory levels and stock availability to prevent overselling and out-of-stock situations, which can lead to order cancellations and returns. Implement inventory management software and reorder triggers to optimize inventory levels and ensure product availability for customers.

Dealing with Return Fraud and Abuse

While most customers are honest and genuine, return fraud and abuse can occur in dropshipping businesses, posing risks to profitability and sustainability. Common types of return fraud include:

1. Wardrobing: Customers purchase items with the intent to use or wear them temporarily and then return them for a refund.

2. Switched or Counterfeit Items: Customers return counterfeit or inferior items in place of the original products to receive a refund.

3. Return of Used or Damaged Items: Customers return items that have been used, damaged, or altered beyond the acceptable condition for a refund.

To mitigate the risks of return fraud and abuse, consider implementing the following preventive measures:

1. Enforce Clear Policies: Clearly communicate your returns and refund policies to customers and enforce them consistently to deter fraudulent behavior.

2. Implement Verification Measures: Require proof of purchase, such as order confirmation emails or receipts, to validate return requests and verify the authenticity of returned items.

3. Inspect Returned Items: Thoroughly inspect returned items upon receipt to ensure that they meet the criteria for refunds or exchanges and detect any signs of wear, damage, or tampering

Legal Considerations and Compliance

In the dynamic world of dropshipping, legal considerations and compliance are essential pillars that uphold the integrity and sustainability of your business. This chapter delves into the intricate legal landscape surrounding dropshipping, providing insights, strategies, and best practices to ensure compliance with relevant laws and regulations.

Understanding Legal Considerations in Dropshipping

Operating a dropshipping business entails navigating a myriad of legal considerations, spanning areas such as business formation, intellectual property rights, consumer protection, taxation, and international trade regulations. By addressing these legal aspects proactively, you can mitigate risks, safeguard your business interests, and foster trust and confidence among customers and stakeholders.

1. Business Formation and Structure: Choosing the right legal structure for your dropshipping business is a foundational step that impacts liability, taxation, and governance. Common business structures include sole proprietorships, partnerships, limited liability companies (LLCs), and corporations. Consider consulting with legal and financial professionals to assess the merits of each structure and determine the most suitable option based on your business goals, risk tolerance, and growth aspirations.

2. Intellectual Property Rights: Protecting intellectual property rights is paramount in dropshipping, where branding, product design, and content creation are integral to business success. Trademarks, copyrights, and patents are valuable assets that safeguard your brand identity, creative works, and innovations from infringement and unauthorized use. Conduct thorough research to identify and register your intellectual property assets and enforce your rights through legal measures if necessary.

3. Contractual Agreements: Establishing clear and enforceable contractual agreements with suppliers, manufacturers, and third-party service providers is essential for defining rights, responsibilities, and obligations in dropshipping partnerships. Contracts should address key terms such as product pricing, payment terms, order fulfillment, quality standards, dispute resolution mechanisms, and termination clauses. Seek legal counsel to draft comprehensive and legally binding contracts that protect your interests and mitigate potential conflicts or disputes.

4. Consumer Protection Laws: Adhering to consumer protection laws and regulations is paramount in maintaining trust and credibility with customers and complying with legal requirements governing e-commerce transactions. Key considerations include transparent pricing and advertising practices, accurate product descriptions, honest and timely disclosures, fair return and refund policies, and compliance with data privacy regulations such as the General Data Protection Regulation (GDPR) in the European Union and the California Consumer Privacy Act (CCPA) in the United States.

5. Taxation and Regulatory Compliance: Understanding the tax implications and regulatory requirements applicable to dropshipping businesses is crucial for maintaining compliance and avoiding potential penalties or liabilities. Tax considerations may include sales tax collection and remittance, income tax reporting, value-added tax (VAT) obligations for international sales, and customs duties and import/ export regulations for cross-border transactions. Consult with tax professionals and legal advisers to ensure compliance with local, state, federal, and international tax laws and regulations.

Strategies for Ensuring Legal Compliance in Dropshipping

Navigating the complex legal landscape of dropshipping requires a strategic approach and proactive measures to ensure compliance and mitigate risks effectively. Consider implementing the following strategies and best practices to safeguard your business interests and maintain legal compliance:

1. Conduct Comprehensive Legal Due Diligence: Prioritize legal due diligence to assess potential risks, liabilities, and regulatory requirements associated with your dropshipping business.

Conduct thorough research and analysis of relevant laws, regulations, and industry standards applicable to your business operations, and identify areas for compliance enhancement or risk mitigation.

2. Establish Robust Legal Documentation: Develop and maintain comprehensive legal documentation, including business formation documents, contractual agreements, terms of service, privacy policies, and disclaimers. Ensure that legal documents are drafted clearly, accurately, and in compliance with applicable laws and regulations, and regularly review and update them to reflect changes in your business operations or legal requirements.

3. Educate and Train Your Team: Invest in employee training and education to raise awareness of legal obligations, compliance requirements, and best practices in dropshipping. Provide employees with resources, guidelines, and training programs to enhance their understanding of legal issues and empower them to make informed decisions that align with regulatory standards and ethical principles.

4. Implement Compliance Monitoring and Auditing: Establish robust compliance monitoring and auditing mechanisms to track adherence to legal requirements and identify potential areas of non-compliance or risk exposure. Conduct regular internal audits, reviews, and assessments of business practices, policies, and procedures, and take corrective action as needed to address deficiencies and strengthen compliance measures.

5. Foster Collaboration with Legal Experts: Collaborate with legal professionals, industry experts, and trade associations to stay abreast of legal developments, emerging trends, and best practices in dropshipping. Seek legal advice and guidance on complex legal issues, regulatory compliance matters, and risk management strategies, and leverage their expertise to proactively address legal challenges and opportunities in your business.

6. Embrace a Culture of Compliance and Ethics: Foster a culture of compliance, integrity, and ethics within your dropshipping organization, where legal compliance and ethical conduct are core values upheld by all stakeholders. Lead by example, communicate the importance of legal compliance and ethical behavior to employees and

business partners, and establish mechanisms for reporting and addressing compliance concerns or ethical dilemmas in a transparent and accountable manner.

Conclusion

Legal considerations and compliance are foundational pillars that underpin the success and sustainability of your dropshipping business. By understanding the legal landscape, addressing key legal considerations proactively, and implementing robust compliance strategies and best practices, you can safeguard your business interests, mitigate risks, and build trust and credibility with customers and stakeholders. Prioritize legal compliance as an integral part of your business strategy, and invest in legal resources, expertise, and infrastructure to navigate the complexities of dropshipping and achieve long-term success in the competitive e-commerce landscape.

Chapter 15

Tips for Long-Term Success

In the fast-paced and competitive world of dropshipping, achieving long-term success requires strategic planning, perseverance, and a commitment to continuous improvement. This chapter explores actionable tips, strategies, and insights to help you build a sustainable and thriving dropshipping business that stands the test of time.

1. Prioritize Customer Satisfaction

At the heart of every successful dropshipping business is a focus on customer satisfaction. Prioritize delivering exceptional customer experiences at every touchpoint, from browsing your website to receiving their orders. Respond promptly to inquiries, address concerns with empathy and professionalism, and go above and beyond to exceed customer expectations. By prioritizing customer satisfaction, you can foster loyalty, drive repeat business, and build a positive reputation for your brand.

2. Invest in Product Quality and Selection

The quality and selection of your products play a crucial role in attracting customers and driving sales. Partner with reputable suppliers and manufacturers who offer high-quality products that meet customer expectations. Regularly evaluate your product assortment, identify trending products and niche opportunities, and expand your offerings to cater to diverse customer preferences and market demands. By investing in product quality and selection, you can differentiate your brand, attract a loyal customer base, and maintain a competitive edge in the market.

3. Build a Strong Brand Identity

A strong brand identity sets you apart from competitors and resonates with your target audience. Develop a compelling brand story, mission, and values that reflect your unique value proposition and resonate with your customers' aspirations and beliefs. Invest in branding elements such as logos, packaging, and website design that convey your brand personality and create a memorable and cohesive brand experience. By building a strong brand identity, you can foster emotional connections with customers, instill trust and loyalty, and position your business for long-term success.

4. Embrace Innovation and Adaptability

The e-commerce landscape is constantly evolving, driven by technological advancements, changing consumer behaviors, and market trends. Embrace innovation and adaptability as core principles of your business strategy, and stay agile and responsive to emerging opportunities and challenges. Experiment with new technologies, marketing channels, and business models to stay ahead of the curve and remain competitive in the market. By embracing innovation and adaptability, you can future-proof your business, drive growth, and capitalize on new market trends and opportunities.

5. Focus on Marketing and Brand Building

Effective marketing and brand building are essential for attracting customers, driving traffic to your website, and generating sales. Develop a comprehensive marketing strategy that encompasses a mix of online and offline channels, including social media marketing, search engine optimization (SEO), content marketing, email marketing, and influencer partnerships. Invest in building brand awareness, engaging with your target audience, and nurturing relationships with customers through personalized and targeted marketing campaigns. By focusing on marketing and brand building, you can increase visibility, drive traffic, and accelerate growth for your dropshipping business.

6. Optimize Operational Efficiency

Operational efficiency is critical for maximizing productivity, minimizing costs, and delivering a seamless and streamlined customer experience. Evaluate your business processes and identify areas for improvement, such as order processing, inventory management, and customer support. Leverage technology and automation tools to streamline repetitive tasks, optimize workflows, and eliminate bottlenecks. Continuously monitor and analyze key performance metrics to identify opportunities for optimization and efficiency gains. By optimizing operational efficiency, you can enhance productivity, improve customer satisfaction, and drive profitability for your dropshipping business.

7. Foster Strategic Partnerships

Strategic partnerships can be invaluable for expanding your reach, accessing new markets, and driving growth for your dropshipping business. Collaborate with complementary brands, influencers, and industry stakeholders to tap into their networks, leverage their expertise, and amplify your marketing efforts. Seek out partnerships that align with your brand values and objectives, and explore opportunities for co-marketing campaigns, cross-promotions, and joint ventures. By fostering strategic partnerships, you can extend your reach, increase brand visibility, and unlock new growth opportunities for your business.

8. Monitor Market Trends and Consumer Behavior

Staying informed about market trends and consumer behavior is essential for making informed business decisions and staying ahead of the competition. Monitor industry publications, market research reports, and consumer insights to identify emerging trends, shifting preferences, and evolving market dynamics. Adapt your product offerings, marketing strategies, and business operations in response to changing market conditions and consumer demands. By staying attuned to market trends and consumer behavior, you can anticipate opportunities, mitigate risks, and position your dropshipping business for long-term success.

9. Cultivate a Culture of Continuous Learning

The landscape of e-commerce is constantly evolving, driven by technological advancements, market dynamics, and consumer trends. Cultivate a culture of continuous learning within your organization, where employees are encouraged to seek out new knowledge, develop new skills, and adapt to changing circumstances. Invest in employee training and development programs, provide access to resources and learning opportunities, and foster a collaborative and supportive work environment. By prioritizing continuous learning, you can empower your team to innovate, adapt, and drive growth for your dropshipping business.

10. Stay Committed to Ethical and Sustainable Practices

Ethical and sustainable practices are increasingly important to today's consumers, who are increasingly conscious of the social and environmental impact of their purchasing decisions. Demonstrate your commitment to ethical and sustainable practices by sourcing products from suppliers who adhere to fair labor practices, environmental regulations, and ethical standards. Implement eco-friendly packaging options, reduce waste, and support initiatives that promote social responsibility and environmental stewardship.

By prioritizing ethical and sustainable practices, you can attract socially conscious consumers, build trust and loyalty, and contribute to positive social and environmental outcomes.

Conclusion

Achieving long-term success in dropshipping requires a strategic and holistic approach that encompasses customer satisfaction, product quality, brand building, operational efficiency, strategic partnerships, and a commitment to continuous learning and improvement. By implementing these tips and strategies, you can build a sustainable and thriving dropshipping business that delivers value to customers, fosters loyalty and trust, and withstands the test of time in the competitive e-commerce landscape. Stay focused, stay adaptable, and stay committed to excellence, and you can achieve your goals and realize your vision for long-term success in dropshipping.

Chapter 16

Leveraging Amazon for Dropshipping Success

Amazon, the e-commerce giant, stands as a behemoth in the online retail landscape, offering unparalleled reach, infrastructure, and resources for entrepreneurs and businesses. In this chapter, we'll explore how to leverage Amazon for dropshipping success, tapping into its vast marketplace, fulfillment network, and customer base to drive growth and achieve your business objectives.

Understanding Amazon's Role in Dropshipping

Amazon's role in dropshipping extends beyond being a marketplace; it serves as a comprehensive ecosystem that offers a myriad of opportunities and tools for dropshippers to thrive. From product sourcing and fulfillment to marketing and customer service,

Amazon provides a robust platform and infrastructure that streamlines operations and facilitates business growth.

1. Marketplace: Amazon's marketplace serves as a global platform where sellers can list and sell their products to millions of customers worldwide. With its vast reach and customer base, the Amazon marketplace offers unparalleled exposure and access to a diverse audience of buyers, making it an attractive channel for dropshipping businesses to expand their reach and drive sales.

2. Fulfillment Network: Through Fulfillment by Amazon (FBA), sellers can leverage Amazon's extensive fulfillment network to store, pack, and ship their products to customers. By utilizing FBA, dropshippers can benefit from Amazon's logistical capabilities, including fast and reliable shipping, order tracking, and customer service, while focusing on growing their business and expanding their product catalog.

3. Advertising: Amazon offers robust advertising solutions, including Sponsored Products, Sponsored Brands, and Sponsored Displays, to help sellers increase visibility, drive traffic, and boost sales for their products. By leveraging

Amazon's advertising platform, dropshippers can target relevant keywords, optimize campaigns, and reach potential customers at various stages of the purchase journey.

4. Brand Registry: Amazon Brand Registry provides tools and resources for sellers to protect their brand identity, intellectual property, and product listings on the platform. By enrolling in Brand Registry, dropshippers can access enhanced brand protection features, such as proprietary text and image search, automated brand monitoring, and proactive enforcement against infringement.

5. Analytics and Insights: Amazon offers robust analytics and reporting tools, such as Amazon Seller Central and Amazon Advertising Console, to help sellers track performance, monitor sales metrics, and gain insights into customer behavior and market trends. By analyzing data and metrics, dropshippers can optimize their strategies, identify opportunities for growth, and make data-driven decisions to drive success on the platform.

Strategies for Leveraging Amazon for Dropshipping Success

Leveraging Amazon for dropshipping success requires a strategic approach and a deep understanding of the platform's capabilities and opportunities. By implementing the following strategies, dropshippers can maximize their presence on Amazon, drive sales, and achieve their business objectives:

1. Identify Profitable Niches: Conduct thorough market research to identify profitable niches and product categories with high demand and low-competition on Amazon. Focus on niche products with unique value propositions, competitive pricing, and strong market potential to differentiate your offerings and attract customers.

2. Optimize Product Listings: Optimize product listings to maximize visibility and conversion rates on Amazon. Use relevant keywords, compelling product titles, detailed descriptions, and high-quality images to enhance discoverability and convey value to customers. Leverage Amazon's A+ Content and Enhanced Brand Content features to create rich and engaging product pages that stand out from competitors and drive sales.

3. Utilize Fulfillment by Amazon (FBA): Leverage Fulfillment by Amazon (FBA) to streamline order fulfillment, improve shipping speed, and enhance the customer experience. By utilizing FBA, dropshippers can benefit from Amazon's logistical infrastructure, including warehousing, packing, shipping, and customer service, while focusing on growing their business and expanding their product catalog.

4. Leverage Amazon Advertising: Invest in Amazon advertising to increase visibility, drive traffic, and boost sales for your products. Experiment with different ad formats, targeting options, and bidding strategies to optimize your campaigns for maximum return on investment (ROI). Monitor performance metrics such as click-through rates (CTR), conversion rates, and advertising cost of sales (ACoS) to measure the effectiveness of your campaigns and make data-driven adjustments.

5. Build a Strong Brand Presence: Focus on building a strong brand presence on Amazon to differentiate your products and stand out from competitors. Invest in branding elements such as logos, packaging, and product imagery to create a cohesive and memorable brand identity. Utilize

Amazon Brand Registry to protect your brand assets and enforce your intellectual property rights on the platform.

6. 6. Provide Exceptional Customer Service: Prioritize delivering exceptional customer service to build trust and loyalty with Amazon customers. Respond promptly to inquiries, address concerns with empathy and professionalism, and strive to exceed customer expectations at every touchpoint. Utilize Amazon's customer feedback and review system to gather insights, address issues, and improve the overall customer experience.

7. Monitor Performance and Optimize Strategies: Continuously monitor performance metrics, such as sales, traffic, conversion rates, and customer feedback, to gauge the effectiveness of your strategies and identify areas for improvement. Utilize Amazon's analytics and reporting tools to track performance, identify trends, and make data-driven decisions to optimize your strategies and drive success on the platform.

8. Stay Compliant with Amazon Policies: Familiarize yourself with Amazon's seller policies, guidelines, and terms of service to ensure compliance and mitigate the risk of account suspension

or deactivation. Adhere to Amazon's rules and regulations regarding product listings, pricing, advertising, and customer communication to maintain a positive seller reputation and avoid penalties or sanctions.

Chapter 17

Expanding Your Reach with International Amazon Marketplaces

Expanding your reach beyond domestic borders is a strategic move for any e-commerce business looking to capitalize on global opportunities. Amazon's international marketplaces offer a gateway to reach millions of customers worldwide, presenting immense potential for growth and expansion. In this chapter, we'll explore the strategies, considerations, and best practices for tapping into international Amazon marketplaces and unlocking new opportunities for your dropshipping business.

Understanding International Amazon Marketplaces

Amazon operates a network of international marketplaces spanning multiple countries and regions, each offering unique opportunities and challenges for sellers. Some of the key international Amazon marketplaces include:

1. Amazon.com (United States): As the largest and most mature Amazon marketplace, Amazon.com offers unparalleled reach and potential for sellers looking to tap into the lucrative U.S. market. With millions of active customers and a diverse range of product categories, Amazon.com presents immense opportunities for dropshippers to expand their reach and drive sales.

2. Amazon.co.uk (United Kingdom): Amazon.co.uk serves as the primary marketplace for sellers targeting the United Kingdom and European markets. With its large and affluent customer base, Amazon.co.uk offers a gateway to reach European consumers and capitalize on cross-border e-commerce opportunities.

3. Amazon.ca (Canada): Amazon.ca caters to Canadian customers, offering a wide range of products across various categories. For dropshippers looking to expand into the Canadian market, Amazon.ca provides access to a wealthy and tech-savvy consumer base with strong purchasing power.

4. Amazon.de (Germany), Amazon.fr (France), Amazon.it (Italy), Amazon.es (Spain): Amazon's European marketplaces, including Germany, France, Italy, and Spain, offer opportunities for sellers to reach European consumers and tap into diverse and affluent markets. With a unified European fulfillment network and access to millions of customers, these marketplaces provide a strategic entry point for international expansion.

5. Amazon.co.jp (Japan), Amazon.com.au (Australia), Amazon.com.mx (Mexico), Amazon.in (India): Amazon's international marketplaces in Japan, Australia, Mexico, and India offer opportunities for sellers to enter emerging markets and capitalize on growing consumer demand. With localized platforms, language support, and cultural nuances, these marketplaces present unique challenges and opportunities for international sellers.

Strategies for Expanding to International Amazon Marketplaces

Expanding to international Amazon marketplaces requires careful planning, market research, and strategic execution. By following these strategies and best practices, dropshippers can successfully expand their reach and capitalize on global opportunities:

1. Conduct Market Research: Start by conducting thorough market research to identify target markets with high demand for your products and favorable market conditions. Evaluate factors such as consumer preferences, purchasing behavior, competition, regulatory requirements, and cultural nuances to assess market viability and potential for success.

2. Choose Target Markets Wisely: Prioritize target markets based on their strategic fit, growth potential, and alignment with your business objectives. Consider factors such as market size, competition, purchasing power, logistics infrastructure, and cultural compatibility when selecting target markets for expansion.

3. Localize Your Approach: Adapt your product offerings, marketing strategies, and customer experience to resonate with local audiences in international markets. Consider factors such as language, currency, pricing, shipping options, and cultural preferences when localizing your approach to ensure relevance and appeal to international customers.

4. Optimize Product Listings: Optimize your product listings for international Amazon marketplaces

by translating product titles, descriptions, and keywords into the local language. Tailor product attributes, features, and specifications to meet the preferences and requirements of international customers and ensure compliance with local regulations and standards.

5. Utilize Fulfillment by Amazon (FBA): Leverage Amazon's Fulfillment by Amazon (FBA) program to streamline order fulfillment, improve shipping speed, and enhance the customer experience in international markets. By utilizing FBA, dropshippers can benefit from Amazon's global fulfillment network and logistical expertise, while focusing on growing their business and expanding their international presence.

6. Invest in International Advertising: Invest in international advertising campaigns to increase visibility, drive traffic, and boost sales for your products on international Amazon marketplaces. Utilize Amazon's advertising platform to target relevant keywords, optimize campaigns, and reach potential customers in your target markets. Monitor performance metrics such as click-through rates (CTR), conversion rates, and return on ad

spend (ROAS) to measure the effectiveness of your campaigns and make data-driven adjustments.

7. Provide Multilingual Customer Support: Offer multilingual customer support to assist international customers and address inquiries, concerns, and issues in their preferred language. Provide support channels such as email, live chat, and phone support in multiple languages to accommodate the needs of international customers and enhance the overall customer experience.

8. Monitor Performance and Iterate: Continuously monitor performance metrics, such as sales, traffic, conversion rates, and customer feedback, to gauge the effectiveness of your strategies and identify areas for improvement. Utilize Amazon's analytics and reporting tools to track performance, identify trends, and make data-driven decisions to optimize your strategies and drive success in international markets.

Chapter 18

Effective Social Media Marketing Strategies

In the ever-evolving landscape of digital marketing, social media has emerged as a powerful platform for connecting with audiences, building brand awareness, and driving engagement. For dropshipping businesses, effective social media marketing strategies can be instrumental in reaching target customers, driving traffic to their online stores, and ultimately, increasing sales and revenue. In this chapter, we'll explore in detail the key elements, tactics, and best practices for implementing effective social media marketing strategies for dropshipping businesses.

Understanding the Importance of Social Media Marketing

Social media marketing offers numerous benefits for dropshipping businesses, including:

1. Increased Brand Visibility: Social media platforms provide a vast audience reach, allowing dropshipping businesses to increase their brand visibility and reach potential customers who may not be aware of their products or services.

2. Enhanced Customer Engagement: Social media enables direct interaction with customers, fostering engagement, building relationships, and gathering feedback. Through likes, comments, shares, and direct messages, dropshipping businesses can engage with their audience on a personal level, addressing inquiries, resolving issues, and building brand loyalty.

3. Targeted Advertising: Social media advertising platforms offer advanced targeting options, allowing dropshipping businesses to reach specific audience segments based on demographics, interests, behaviors, and other criteria. By targeting the right audience with relevant ads, businesses can maximize their return on investment (ROI) and drive conversions.

4. Content Distribution: Social media serves as a powerful distribution channel for content, enabling dropshipping businesses to share product updates, promotions, blog posts, videos, and other content

formats with their audience. By creating valuable and engaging content, businesses can attract, educate, and inspire their audience, driving traffic to their online stores and increasing brand awareness.

5. Data Analytics and Insights: Social media platforms provide robust analytics and insights tools that allow businesses to track performance metrics, measure the effectiveness of their campaigns, and gain valuable insights into audience behavior and preferences. By analyzing data and metrics, businesses can optimize their strategies, refine their targeting, and improve their results over time.

Effective Social Media Marketing Strategies for Dropshipping Businesses

To leverage the power of social media effectively, dropshipping businesses can implement the following strategies and best practices:

1. Define Your Goals and Objectives: Start by defining clear and measurable goals for your social media marketing efforts. Whether it's increasing brand awareness, driving website traffic, generating

leads, or boosting sales, having clear objectives will guide your strategy and help you measure success.

2. Know Your Audience: Understand your target audience's demographics, interests, behaviors, and preferences to tailor your content and messaging effectively. Conduct audience research, analyze social media insights, and engage with your audience to gain insights into their needs, challenges, and aspirations.

3. Choose the Right Platforms: Select social media platforms that align with your target audience and business objectives. While Facebook, Instagram, and Twitter are popular choices for most businesses, consider niche platforms such as Pinterest, LinkedIn, TikTok, or Snapchat if they resonate with your audience and industry.

4. Create Compelling Content: Develop high-quality, relevant, and engaging content that resonates with your audience and adds value to their lives. Experiment with different content formats, such as images, videos, infographics, blog posts, and user-generated content, to keep your audience engaged and entertained.

5. Develop a Content Calendar: Plan and organize your social media content in advance using a content calendar. Schedule regular posts, promotions, and campaigns to maintain consistency and keep your audience engaged. Be mindful of key dates, holidays, and events that are relevant to your audience and industry.

6. Leverage Visuals and Multimedia: Visual content tends to perform better on social media, so incorporate eye-catching images, videos, and graphics into your posts and ads. Use professional photography, compelling visuals, and branded imagery to capture attention and convey your brand identity effectively.

7. Engage and Interact with Your Audience: Actively engage with your audience by responding to comments, messages, and mentions in a timely and authentic manner. Foster two-way conversations, ask questions, solicit feedback, and encourage user-generated content to build rapport and strengthen relationships with your audience.

8. Utilize Influencer Marketing: Collaborate with influencers, bloggers, and content creators in your niche to amplify your reach and credibility on social media. Identify influencers with relevant audiences

and authentic engagement, and partner with them to create sponsored content, host giveaways, or co-create product reviews and tutorials.

9. Run Targeted Advertising Campaigns: Utilize social media advertising platforms to run targeted ad campaigns that reach your ideal audience effectively. Define your target audience, set clear objectives, and create compelling ad creatives and copy that drive action. Monitor campaign performance, optimize targeting, and adjust budgets and bids to maximize ROI.

10. Track and Measure Results: Monitor key performance metrics such as engagement, reach, clicks, conversions, and return on ad spend (ROAS) to evaluate the effectiveness of your social media marketing efforts. Use social media analytics tools and platform insights to track performance, identify trends, and make data-driven decisions to optimize your strategy.

Chapter 19

Utilizing Influencer Marketing for Brand Awareness

In today's digital age, influencer marketing has emerged as a powerful strategy for brands to reach and engage with their target audience authentically. Leveraging the influence and credibility of social media personalities, influencers can help brands amplify their message, build brand awareness, and drive engagement. For dropshipping businesses, influencer marketing presents a valuable opportunity to connect with potential customers, increase brand visibility, and, ultimately, boost sales and revenue. In this chapter, we'll delve into the intricacies of influencer marketing, exploring its benefits, strategies, and best practices for effectively leveraging influencers to enhance brand awareness and drive success.

Understanding Influencer Marketing

Influencer marketing involves collaborating with individuals who have a significant following and influence on social media platforms to promote products or services. These influencers, often referred to as content creators, bloggers, or social media personalities, have built a loyal and engaged audience around specific niches, topics, or interests. By partnering with influencers, brands can tap into their reach, credibility, and rapport with their audience to endorse products, share recommendations, and drive engagement.

Key Elements of Influencer Marketing

1. Influencer Identification: The first step in influencer marketing is identifying relevant influencers who align with your brand values, target audience, and marketing objectives. Consider factors such as audience demographics, engagement metrics, content quality, and niche relevance when evaluating potential influencers for collaboration.

2. Campaign Strategy: Develop a clear and strategic campaign strategy that outlines your objectives, target audience, messaging, and desired outcomes. Determine the type of content you

want influencers to create, whether it's sponsored posts, product reviews, tutorials, giveaways, or endorsements, and establish guidelines and expectations for collaboration.

3. Relationship Building: Cultivate genuine relationships with influencers based on mutual respect, trust, and transparency. Reach out to influencers with personalized messages, express interest in their content, and demonstrate an understanding of their audience and niche. Collaborate closely with influencers to co-create content, provide support and resources, and ensure alignment with your brand values and objectives.

4. Content Creation: Work collaboratively with influencers to create compelling and authentic content that resonates with their audience and aligns with your brand messaging. Provide clear guidelines, creative direction, and brand assets, but allow influencers creative freedom to infuse their personality and style into the content. Ensure that sponsored content is clearly disclosed and complies with relevant advertising regulations and guidelines.

5. Campaign Execution: Execute your influencer marketing campaigns effectively by coordinating timelines, deliverables, and promotional activities with influencers. Monitor campaign progress, provide feedback and support as needed, and track key performance metrics such as reach, engagement, clicks, and conversions to evaluate campaign effectiveness and ROI.

6. Performance Measurement: Measure the performance of your influencer marketing campaigns using relevant metrics and analytics tools. Analyze engagement rates, follower growth, website traffic, conversion rates, and sales attribution to assess the impact of influencer collaborations on your brand awareness, reach, and bottom line. Use insights gleaned from performance data to refine your strategy, optimize future campaigns, and drive continuous improvement.

Benefits of Influencer Marketing for Dropshipping Businesses

1. Increased Brand Visibility: Partnering with influencers allows dropshipping businesses to expand their reach and increase brand visibility

among target audiences who may not be familiar with their products or services. By leveraging the influencer's existing audience and credibility, brands can amplify their message and generate awareness more effectively than traditional marketing channels.

2. Authenticity and Trust: Influencers often have a close and authentic relationship with their audience, built on trust, transparency, and authenticity. When influencers endorse products or services, their recommendations are perceived as genuine and trustworthy, leading to higher levels of engagement and conversion among their followers.

3. Targeted Reach: Influencers typically cater to specific niches, interests, or demographics, allowing brands to reach highly targeted and relevant audiences. By partnering with influencers whose audience aligns with their target market, dropshipping businesses can ensure that their message resonates with the right audience, increasing the likelihood of engagement and conversion.

4. Content Creation: Influencers are skilled content creators who excel at producing high-quality and

engaging content that captures the attention of their audience. By collaborating with influencers, dropshipping businesses can leverage their creativity, expertise, and storytelling abilities to create compelling branded content that drives engagement, educates consumers, and enhances brand perception.

5. Cost-Effective Marketing: Compared to traditional advertising channels, influencer marketing can be a cost-effective way for dropshipping businesses to reach their target audience and drive results. Instead of investing significant resources in paid advertising or sponsored content, brands can leverage the reach and influence of influencers at a fraction of the cost, making it an attractive option for businesses with limited marketing budgets.

Chapter 20

Implementing Email Marketing Campaigns

Email marketing remains one of the most powerful and effective tools in a marketer's arsenal, offering unparalleled reach, engagement, and ROI for businesses of all sizes. For dropshipping businesses, email marketing presents a valuable opportunity to nurture relationships with customers, drive repeat purchases, and increase lifetime value. In this chapter, we'll explore the intricacies of email marketing, from crafting compelling campaigns to leveraging automation and analytics to drive success.

Understanding the Power of Email Marketing

Email marketing is a digital marketing strategy that involves sending targeted and personalized emails to a list of subscribers with the aim of nurturing relationships, promoting products or services, and driving conversions. With its ability to deliver highly targeted messages directly to subscribers' inboxes, email marketing enables businesses to engage with their audience in a more intimate and personalized way, driving engagement, loyalty, and sales.

Key Benefits of Email Marketing for Dropshipping Businesses

1. Direct Communication Channel: Email provides a direct line of communication between businesses and their customers, allowing for personalized and targeted messaging. By delivering messages directly to subscribers' inboxes, businesses can cut through the noise of other marketing channels and capture the attention of their audience more effectively.

2. Relationship Building: Email marketing enables dropshipping businesses to build and nurture relationships with their audience over time. By delivering valuable and relevant content, providing personalized recommendations, and offering exclusive deals and promotions, businesses can strengthen their connection with customers and foster loyalty and trust.

3. Cost-Effective Marketing: Email marketing is a cost-effective way for dropshipping businesses to reach their audience and drive results. Compared to traditional advertising channels, such as print or TV ads, email marketing offers a lower cost per acquisition (CPA) and a higher return on investment (ROI), making it an attractive option for businesses with limited marketing budgets.

4. Targeted Messaging: Email marketing allows businesses to segment their audience and send targeted messages based on factors such as demographics, purchase history, interests, and behaviors. By tailoring content and offers to specific segments of their audience, businesses can deliver more relevant and personalized messages that resonate with recipients and drive engagement and conversions.

5. Measurable Results: Email marketing offers robust analytics and tracking capabilities that allow businesses to measure the performance of their campaigns in real time. From open rates and click-through rates to conversion rates and revenue attribution, businesses can track key metrics to gauge the effectiveness of their email marketing

efforts and make data-driven decisions to optimize their strategy.

Implementing Effective Email Marketing Campaigns

1. Build a Quality Email List: The foundation of successful email marketing is a quality email list comprised of engaged and interested subscribers. Start by collecting email addresses through opt-in forms on your website, blog, and social media channels. Offer incentives such as discounts, freebies, or exclusive content to encourage sign-ups and attract subscribers who are genuinely interested in your products or services.

2. Segment Your Audience: Segment your email list based on factors such as demographics, purchase history, engagement level, and preferences. By segmenting your audience into smaller, more targeted groups, you can deliver more relevant and personalized messages that resonate with recipients and drive higher engagement and conversions.

3. Personalize Your Emails: Personalization is key to effective email marketing. Use the recipient's name, past purchase history, browsing behavior,

and other relevant data points to personalize your emails and make them feel more relevant and tailored to each recipient. Personalized emails are more likely to capture attention, drive engagement, and compel recipients to take action.

4. Create Compelling Content: Invest in creating high-quality and engaging content that provides value to your subscribers. Whether it's informative blog posts, product updates, how-to guides, or exclusive offers, ensure that your content is relevant, timely, and valuable to your audience. Use compelling subject lines, eye-catching visuals, and clear calls-to-action to encourage opens, clicks, and conversions.

5. Optimize for Mobile: With the majority of emails being opened on mobile devices, it's essential to optimize your emails for mobile responsiveness. Ensure that your emails are mobile-friendly and render correctly on a variety of devices and screen sizes. Use responsive design principles, single-column layouts, and large, tappable buttons to create a seamless and intuitive mobile experience for recipients.

6. Automate Your Campaigns: Take advantage of email automation tools and workflows to streamline

your email marketing efforts and save time. Set up automated campaigns such as welcome emails, abandoned cart reminders, post-purchase follow-ups, and re-engagement campaigns to deliver relevant messages to subscribers at the right time in their customer journey.

7. Test and Iterate: Continuously test and optimize your email marketing campaigns to maximize their effectiveness and impact. Experiment with different subject lines, send times, content formats, and calls-to-action to identify what resonates best with your audience. Use A/B testing and multivariate testing to compare different variables and determine which elements drive the highest engagement and conversions.

8. Monitor and Analyze Results: Track key performance metrics such as open rates, click-through rates, conversion rates, and revenue attribution to measure the success of your email marketing campaigns. Use email analytics and reporting tools to gain insights into recipient behavior, identify trends, and make data-driven decisions to optimize your strategy and drive better results.

Chapter 21

Understanding SEO for E-commerce

In the digital landscape of e-commerce, search engine optimization (SEO) stands as a critical component for driving organic traffic, increasing visibility, and, ultimately, boosting sales and revenue. For e-commerce businesses, mastering the intricacies of SEO is essential to outshine competitors, rank higher in search engine results pages (SERPs), and attract qualified leads and customers. In this chapter, we'll embark on a comprehensive journey through the realm of SEO for e-commerce, unraveling its principles, strategies, and best practices for achieving success in the competitive online marketplace.

Understanding the Fundamentals of SEO

Search engine optimization (SEO) is the practice of optimizing your website to improve its visibility and ranking in search engine results for relevant keywords and queries. In the context of e-commerce, SEO encompasses various strategies and tactics aimed at enhancing the online presence of e-commerce websites, driving organic traffic, and increasing conversions and sales.

Key Components of E-commerce SEO

1. On-Page SEO: On-page SEO focuses on optimizing individual web pages to improve their relevance, authority, and visibility in search engine results. Key elements of on-page SEO for e-commerce include:

   - Keyword Research: Identify relevant keywords and phrases that potential customers are using to search for products or services in your niche. Use keyword research tools to discover high-volume, low-competition keywords with commercial intent.

   - Title Tags and Meta Descriptions: Optimize title tags and meta descriptions to include target keywords and entice users to click through to your website. Craft compelling, descriptive, and relevant titles and meta descriptions that accurately reflect the content of the page.

- Product Descriptions: Write unique, informative, and keyword-rich product descriptions that highlight the features, benefits, and unique selling points of your products. Avoid duplicate content and strive to provide valuable and engaging content that helps customers make informed purchasing decisions.

- URL Structure: Create SEO-friendly URLs that are descriptive, concise, and keyword-rich. Use hyphens to separate words, avoid unnecessary parameters or session IDs, and include relevant keywords in the URL to improve search engine visibility and readability.

- Image Optimization: Optimize product images for search engines by using descriptive filenames, alt text, and captions. Include relevant keywords in alt text and captions to improve image visibility in search engine image results and enhance accessibility for visually impaired users.

2. Technical SEO: Technical SEO focuses on optimizing the technical aspects of your website to improve its crawlability, indexability, and performance in search engines. Key elements of technical SEO for e-commerce include:

   - Site Speed: Improve website speed and performance by optimizing page load times, minimizing server response times, and leveraging browser caching. Use tools like Google Page Speed Insights and GTmetrix to identify and address performance issues.

   - Mobile Optimization: Ensure that your e-commerce website is mobile-friendly and responsive across various devices and screen sizes. Implement responsive design principles, use mobile-friendly fonts and buttons, and prioritize mobile user experience to cater to the growing number of mobile users.

   - Site Structure: Create a logical and intuitive site structure that allows users and search engines to navigate your website easily. Organize products into categories and subcategories, use breadcrumb navigation for hierarchical organization, and ensure that internal links are properly implemented to facilitate crawling and indexing.

- Schema Markup: Implement schema markup to provide search engines with additional context and information about your products, such as product name, price, availability, and ratings. Use structured data markup formats like JSON-LD or Microdata to enhance search engine visibility and enrich search results with rich snippets.

- XML Sitemap: Create an XML sitemap that lists all the pages and products on your e-commerce website and submit it to search engines like Google and Bing. A sitemap helps search engines discover and crawl your website more efficiently, ensuring that all your pages are indexed and included in search results.

3. Off-Page SEO: Off-page SEO involves optimizing external factors that impact your website's authority, relevance, and credibility in search engines. Key elements of off-page SEO for e-commerce include:

- Link Building: Acquire high-quality backlinks from authoritative and relevant websites to improve your website's authority and trustworthiness in the eyes of search engines. Focus on earning natural and organic backlinks through content marketing, guest blogging, influencer outreach, and digital PR.

- Social Signals: Leverage social media platforms to amplify your e-commerce brand and generate social signals that indicate authority and relevance to search engines. Encourage social sharing, likes, comments, and engagement on social media to increase brand visibility and drive traffic to your website.

- Online Reviews and Reputation Management: Monitor and manage online reviews and ratings of your e-commerce business to build trust and credibility with potential customers. Encourage satisfied customers to leave positive reviews and address negative reviews promptly and professionally to mitigate reputational damage.

4. Content Marketing: Content marketing plays a crucial role in e-commerce SEO by providing

valuable, informative, and engaging content that attracts and engages target audiences. Key content marketing strategies for e-commerce include:

- Blogging: Create a blog on your e-commerce website to publish informative articles, how-to guides, product reviews, and industry insights. Use blogging to target long-tail keywords, answer common questions, and educate and inform potential customers.

- Product Guides and Tutorials: Create comprehensive product guides, tutorials, and instructional videos that showcase the features, benefits, and use cases of your products. Provide valuable and practical information that helps customers make informed purchasing decisions and encourages them to engage with your brand.

- User-Generated Content: Encourage user-generated content such as product reviews, testimonials, and social media mentions to increase social proof and authenticity. Showcase user-generated content on your website and social media channels to build trust and credibility with potential customers.

5. Local SEO: For brick-and-mortar e-commerce businesses with physical locations, local SEO is essential for increasing visibility and attracting local customers. Key elements of local SEO for e-commerce include:

- Google My Business: Claim and optimize your Google My Business listing to ensure accurate business information, including name, address, phone number, and hours of operation. Encourage customers to leave reviews and ratings on your Google My Business profile to improve local search visibility.

- Local Citations: Ensure that your business information is consistent and accurate across online directories, review sites, and local listings. Build local citations on authoritative directories such as Yelp, Yellow Pages, and TripAdvisor to improve local search rankings and increase visibility in local search results.

- Local Content and Outreach: Create locally relevant content, such as blog posts, articles, and event announcements, to target local keywords and attract local customers. Partner with local businesses, organizations, and influencers to increase your brand's visibility and reach within the local community.

Implementing E-commerce SEO Strategies

1. Conduct Keyword Research: Start by conducting keyword research to identify relevant keywords and phrases that potential customers are using to search for products or services in your niche. Use keyword research tools like Google Keyword Planner, SEMrush, or Ahrefs to discover high-volume, low-competition keywords with commercial intent.

2. Optimize Product Pages: Optimize your e-commerce product pages for target keywords and user intent. Use descriptive and keyword-rich product titles, headings, and meta descriptions to improve search engine visibility and attract clicks from search engine users. Incorporate relevant keywords naturally throughout the page content, including product descriptions, bullet points, and image alt text.

3. Improve Site Structure and Navigation: Create a logical and intuitive site structure that allows users and search engines to navigate your e-commerce

website easily. Organize products into categories and subcategories, use breadcrumb navigation for hierarchical organization, and ensure that internal links are properly implemented to facilitate crawling and indexing.

4. Optimize Page Load Speed: Improve the speed and performance of your e-commerce website by optimizing page load times, minimizing server response times, and leveraging browser caching. Use tools like Google PageSpeed Insights, GTmetrix, or Pingdom to identify and address performance issues, such as large image files, render-blocking scripts, or server bottlenecks.

5. Implement Schema Markup: Implement schema markup to provide search engines with additional context and information about your products, such as product name, price, availability, and ratings. Use structured data markup formats like JSON-LD or Microdata to enhance search engine visibility and enrich search results with rich snippets, such as product ratings, reviews, and pricing information.

6. Create High-Quality Content: Invest in creating high-quality and informative content that provides value to your target audience. Publish blog posts, articles, how-to guides, and product reviews that

target relevant keywords and address common questions and pain points of your target customers. Use multimedia content such as images, videos, and infographics to enhance engagement and shareability.

7. Build High-Quality Backlinks: Acquire high-quality backlinks from authoritative and relevant websites to improve your website's authority and credibility in the eyes of search engines. Focus on earning natural and organic backlinks through content marketing, guest blogging, influencer outreach, and digital PR. Avoid low-quality and spammy backlinks that can harm your website's reputation and rankings.

8. Optimize for Mobile: Ensure that your e-commerce website is mobile-friendly and responsive across various devices and screen sizes. Implement responsive design principles, use mobile-friendly fonts and buttons, and prioritize mobile user experience to cater to the growing number of mobile users and improve search engine rankings in mobile search results.

9. Monitor Performance and Analytics: Track key performance metrics such as organic traffic, keyword rankings, conversion rates, and revenue

attribution to measure the effectiveness of your e-commerce SEO efforts. Use tools like Google Analytics, Google Search Console, and third-party SEO platforms to monitor performance, identify opportunities, and make data-driven decisions to optimize your strategy and drive better results.

Chapter 22

Analyzing and Optimizing Conversion Rates

In the dynamic world of e-commerce, conversion rate optimization (CRO) stands as a cornerstone for driving profitability, maximizing revenue, and enhancing the overall success of online businesses. By meticulously analyzing user behavior, identifying pain points, and implementing strategic optimizations, e-commerce entrepreneurs can unlock the full potential of their websites and turn visitors into loyal customers. In this chapter, we'll embark on a comprehensive exploration of conversion rate analysis and optimization strategies, delving into the intricacies of user experience, persuasive design, and data-driven decision-making.

Understanding Conversion Rate Optimization (CRO)

Conversion rate optimization (CRO) is the process of systematically improving the performance of a website or landing page to increase the percentage of visitors who take a desired action, such as making a purchase, signing up for a newsletter, or requesting a quote. By optimizing key elements of the user experience, addressing barriers to conversion, and testing hypotheses through A/B testing and experimentation, businesses can drive incremental improvements in conversion rates and achieve their objectives more effectively.

Key Components of Conversion Rate Optimization

1. User Experience (UX) Optimization: User experience plays a crucial role in conversion rate optimization, as it directly impacts how visitors interact with your website and navigate through the conversion funnel. Key elements of UX optimization for e-commerce include:

   - Intuitive Navigation: Ensure that your website has clear, intuitive navigation that guides visitors seamlessly through the browsing and checkout process. Use logical navigation menus, breadcrumb trails, and internal links to help users find what they're looking for quickly and easily.

- Mobile Responsiveness: With the increasing prevalence of mobile devices, it's essential to optimize your website for mobile responsiveness. Ensure that your website is fully responsive across all devices and screen sizes, with easy-to-tap buttons, readable text, and fast-loading pages.

- Page Speed Optimization: Improve page load times and overall website performance to minimize bounce rates and increase engagement. Optimize images, enable browser caching, and minimize server response times to create a smooth and seamless user experience.

- Streamlined Checkout Process: Simplify the checkout process and remove any unnecessary friction points that may deter users from completing their purchase. Implement a guest checkout option, offer multiple payment methods, and minimize form fields to streamline the checkout experience.

- Clear Call-to-Action (CTA): Use clear and compelling calls-to-action (CTAs) throughout your website to guide users toward desired actions. Use contrasting colors, persuasive copy, and strategic placement to make CTAs stand out and encourage clicks and conversions.

2. Persuasive Design Elements: Persuasive design elements can significantly impact conversion rates by influencing user behavior and decision-making. Key persuasive design elements for e-commerce include:

- Social Proof: Incorporate social proof elements such as customer reviews, testimonials, ratings, and endorsements to build trust and credibility with potential customers. Highlight positive feedback and user-generated content to reassure visitors and alleviate concerns.

- Scarcity and Urgency: Create a sense of urgency and scarcity to encourage visitors to take action quickly. Use countdown timers, limited-time offers, and low-stock notifications to create a fear of missing out (FOMO) and prompt users to make a purchase before it's too late.

- Trust Signals: Display trust signals such as security badges, SSL certificates, and payment logos prominently on your website to reassure visitors about the safety and reliability of their transactions. Highlight your privacy policy, return policy, and customer support options to build trust and confidence.

- Visual Hierarchy: Use visual hierarchy to guide users' attention toward key elements and CTAs on your website. Use size, color, contrast, and placement to create a clear and intuitive hierarchy of information that directs users toward conversion goals.

- Personalization: Personalize the user experience by tailoring content, recommendations, and offers based on user preferences, behavior, and past interactions. Use data-driven personalization techniques to create a more relevant and engaging experience that resonates with individual users.

3. Data-Driven Optimization Techniques: Data-driven optimization techniques involve analyzing user data, conducting experiments, and iteratively testing and refining hypotheses to improve conversion rates. Key data-driven optimization techniques for e-commerce include:

- A/B Testing: Conduct A/B tests to compare different variations of website elements, such as headlines, CTAs, images, and layouts, to determine which version performs better in terms of conversions. Use statistical analysis to identify winning variations and implement changes accordingly.

- Multivariate Testing: Conduct multivariate tests to analyze the combined impact of multiple variables on conversion rates. Test different combinations of elements simultaneously to identify the most effective combinations for driving conversions.

- Heatmaps and Click Tracking: Use heatmaps and click tracking tools to visualize user behavior and interaction patterns on your website. Identify areas of high engagement, as well as areas of friction or drop-off, and use this data to inform optimization efforts.

- Conversion Funnel Analysis: Analyze your website's conversion funnel to identify bottlenecks, drop-off points, and areas for improvement. Use tools like Google Analytics to track user behavior throughout the conversion process and identify opportunities for optimization.

- User Surveys and Feedback: Collect user feedback through surveys, polls, and feedback forms to gain insights into user preferences, pain points, and expectations. Use qualitative data to supplement quantitative analysis and inform optimization strategies based on user insights.

4. Continuous Optimization and Iteration: Conversion rate optimization is an ongoing process that requires continuous monitoring, testing, and iteration to achieve optimal results. Develop a culture of experimentation and optimization within your organization, and prioritize ongoing testing and refinement of website elements to drive continuous improvement.

Implementing Conversion Rate Optimization Strategies

1. Identify Conversion Goals: Start by identifying clear and measurable conversion goals for your e-commerce website. Whether it's increasing product purchases, newsletter sign-ups, or demo requests, define specific conversion actions that align with your business objectives and KPIs.

2. Conduct Conversion Audits: Conduct a thorough audit of your website to identify areas for improvement and optimization. Analyze key conversion metrics, such as conversion rate, bounce rate, and average order value, and identify potential pain points or barriers to conversion.

3. Develop Hypotheses: Based on your conversion audit and analysis, develop hypotheses for optimization experiments. Formulate hypotheses that address specific issues or opportunities identified during the audit and propose potential solutions or changes to test.

4. Prioritize Optimization Efforts: Prioritize optimization efforts based on potential impact, feasibility, and resource requirements. Focus on high-impact areas that are likely to have a

significant effect on conversion rates and allocate resources accordingly.

5. Implement A/B Tests: Implement A/B tests to compare different variations of website elements and measure their impact on conversion rates. Test variations of headlines, CTAs, product descriptions, pricing strategies, and other key elements to identify winning variations.

6. Analyze Results: Analyze the results of your A/B ests using statistical analysis to determine which variations perform best in terms of conversions. Identify winning variations and implement changes accordingly while also documenting key learnings and insights for future optimization efforts.

7. Iterate and Refine: Iterate and refine your optimization strategies based on test results and insights gleaned from experimentation. Continuously monitor performance metrics, conduct additional tests, and refine your hypotheses to drive ongoing improvements in conversion rates.

8. Monitor Performance: Monitor the performance of your website and conversion funnel on an ongoing basis to track progress and identify areas

for further optimization. Use tools like Google Analytics, heatmaps, and user feedback to gain insights into user behavior and inform optimization strategies.

Chapter 23

Google Ads for Targeted Advertising

In the realm of digital marketing, Google Ads stands as a powerful and versatile platform for reaching targeted audiences, driving traffic, and achieving business objectives. With its extensive reach, robust targeting capabilities, and flexible ad formats, Google Ads empowers advertisers to connect with potential customers at every stage of the buyer's journey and drive measurable results. In this chapter, we'll explore the intricacies of Google Ads for targeted advertising, uncovering strategies, best practices, and optimization techniques for maximizing the effectiveness of your campaigns.

Understanding Google Ads

Google Ads, formerly known as Google AdWords, is an online advertising platform developed by Google that allows advertisers to display ads on Google's search engine results pages (SERPs), as well as on its network of partner websites and platforms. Google Ads operates on a pay-per-click (PPC) model, where advertisers bid on keywords and pay for ad clicks, impressions, or conversions.

Key Components of Google Ads:

1. Ad Campaigns: Ad campaigns are the foundation of Google Ads, allowing advertisers to organize and manage their advertising efforts around specific goals, audiences, and budgets. Each campaign can contain multiple ad groups, each targeting a different set of keywords or audience segments.

2. Ad Groups: Ad groups are subsets of campaigns that contain a set of related keywords, ads, and targeting criteria. Advertisers can create multiple ad groups within a campaign to target different themes, products, or audience segments, allowing for more granular control and optimization.

3. Keywords: Keywords are the search terms or phrases that trigger your ads to appear in Google search results. Advertisers can bid on specific keywords relevant to their products or services

and create ads that appear when users search for those keywords on Google.

4. Ad Formats: Google Ads offers a variety of ad formats and extensions to help advertisers capture users' attention and drive engagement. Common ad formats include text ads, display ads, video ads, shopping ads, and app promotion ads, each tailored to different campaign objectives and audience preferences.

5. Targeting Options: Google Ads provides robust targeting options to help advertisers reach their desired audience with precision and accuracy. Targeting options include geographic targeting, demographic targeting, audience targeting, device targeting, and remarketing, allowing advertisers to tailor their ads to specific audiences based on their characteristics and behaviors.

6. Bidding Strategies: Bidding strategies determine how advertisers pay for ad placements and optimize their campaigns for specific goals, such as clicks, conversions, or impressions. Google Ads offers a range of bidding strategies, including manual bidding, automated bidding, and performance-based bidding, each suited to different campaign objectives and budgets.

7. Ad Auction: Google Ads uses an auction-based system to determine which ads appear on its search results pages and partner websites. Advertisers bid on keywords and compete for ad placements based on factors such as bid amount, ad relevance, and ad quality score, with the highest-quality and most relevant ads winning the top positions.

Creating Targeted Google Ads Campaigns

1. Define Your Campaign Objectives: Start by defining clear and measurable objectives for your Google Ads campaigns, such as driving website traffic, generating leads, increasing sales, or promoting brand awareness. Align your campaign objectives with your overall business goals and KPIs to ensure that your advertising efforts are focused and purposeful.

2. Conduct Keyword Research: Conduct keyword research to identify relevant keywords and phrases that potential customers are using to search for products or services in your niche. Use keyword research tools like Google Keyword Planner, SEMrush, or Ahrefs to discover high-volume, low-competition keywords with commercial intent.

3. Structure Your Campaigns and Ad Groups: Organize your Google Ads campaigns and ad groups in a logical and hierarchical structure that reflects your business goals and target audience segments. Create separate campaigns for different products, services, or marketing objectives, and divide each campaign into ad groups based on themes, product categories, or keyword themes.

4. Choose Targeting Options: Choose targeting options that allow you to reach your desired audience with precision and accuracy. Consider factors such as geographic location, demographic characteristics, audience interests, and device preferences when setting targeting criteria for your ads. Use audience targeting options such as demographics, interests, and remarketing to reach specific audience segments with tailored messaging and offers.

5. Craft Compelling Ad Copy: Craft compelling and persuasive ad copy that grabs users' attention, communicates your value proposition, and encourages them to take action. Use clear and concise language, highlight key benefits and features, and include a strong call-to-action (CTA) that prompts users to click on your ad.

6. Create Relevant Landing Pages: Create relevant and engaging landing pages that align with your ad copy and offer a seamless and intuitive user experience. Ensure that landing pages are optimized for conversion, with clear messaging, compelling visuals, and prominent calls-to-action that guide users toward desired actions.

7. Set Bidding Strategies: Set bidding strategies that align with your campaign objectives and budget constraints. Choose bidding strategies based on your desired outcome, whether it's maximizing clicks, conversions, or impressions, and adjust bid amounts and bid adjustments to optimize performance and achieve your goals.

8. Monitor and Optimize Performance: Monitor the performance of your Google Ads campaigns on an ongoing basis and make data-driven optimizations to improve results. Track key metrics such as click-through rate (CTR), conversion rate, cost per conversion, and return on ad spend (ROAS), and adjust campaign settings, targeting criteria, and ad creatives based on performance insights.

Advanced Google Ads Strategies for Targeted Advertising

1. Dynamic Search Ads (DSA): Dynamic Search Ads (DSA) automatically generate ad headlines and landing page URLs based on the content of your website and the search queries of users. DSA campaigns are particularly effective for e-commerce businesses with large product catalogs or frequently changing inventory, as they allow advertisers to target a wide range of search queries dynamically.

2. Remarketing and Retargeting: Remarketing and retargeting campaigns allow advertisers to re-engage users who have previously visited their website or interacted with their brand. By targeting users with personalized ads based on their past interactions and behaviors, remarketing campaigns can help drive conversions, increase brand awareness, and foster customer loyalty.

3. Local Ads and Local Extensions: Local ads and local extensions allow advertisers to target users based on their geographic location and proximity to their business locations. Displaying relevant information such as store hours, directions, and contact information, as well as local ads and extensions,

can help drive foot traffic to physical locations and increase sales for brick-and-mortar businesses.

4. Smart Bidding and Automated Optimization: Smart bidding and automated optimization techniques leverage machine learning and AI algorithms to optimize bidding strategies and campaign performance automatically. By analyzing vast amounts of data in real time, smart bidding algorithms can adjust bid amounts, targeting criteria, and ad placements to maximize results and achieve campaign objectives more efficiently.

5. Video and Display Ads: Video and display ads allow advertisers to engage users with visually compelling and interactive content across Google's network of partner websites, YouTube, and other online platforms. Video ads are particularly effective for storytelling, brand building, and product demonstrations, while display ads can help increase brand visibility, drive website traffic, and generate leads.

Chapter 24

Alternative Marketplaces (E.g., EBay, Etsy)

In the ever-evolving landscape of e-commerce, alternative marketplaces offer diverse opportunities for sellers to expand their reach, connect with niche audiences, and diversify their sales channels beyond traditional platforms like Amazon and Shopify. From eBay's bustling auction marketplace to Etsy's artisanal community of makers and creators, alternative marketplaces cater to a wide range of products, industries, and consumer preferences. In this chapter, we'll delve into the world of alternative marketplaces, exploring the unique features, benefits, and best practices for selling on platforms like eBay, Etsy, and more.

Understanding Alternative Marketplaces

Alternative marketplaces, also known as online marketplaces, are digital platforms that facilitate the buying and selling of goods and services between independent sellers and consumers. Unlike traditional e-commerce platforms, which typically focus on retailing new products from established brands, alternative marketplaces often emphasize unique or handmade products, vintage items, collectibles, and personalized goods.

Key Characteristics of Alternative Marketplaces

1. Diverse Product Offerings: Alternative marketplaces feature a diverse range of products spanning various categories, industries, and niches. From handmade crafts and vintage clothing to rare collectibles and custom artwork, alternative marketplaces cater to a wide range of consumer preferences and interests.

2. Independent Sellers: Alternative marketplaces provide a platform for independent sellers, artisans, and small businesses to showcase their products and reach a global audience. Sellers can create their own storefronts, list products for sale,

and manage transactions directly with customers, often without the need for a middleman or intermediary.

3. Unique Shopping Experience: Alternative marketplaces offer a unique and immersive shopping experience characterized by personalized recommendations, curated collections, and community engagement. Many platforms prioritize discovery and exploration, allowing users to browse through curated collections, follow favorite sellers, and interact with like-minded enthusiasts.

4. Seller-Friendly Policies: Alternative marketplaces typically offer seller-friendly policies and terms, including low fees, flexible listing options, and transparent selling practices. Sellers often have greater control over pricing, inventory management, and customer communication, empowering them to build and grow their businesses on their own terms.

5. Community Engagement: Alternative marketplaces foster a sense of community and belonging among buyers and sellers, encouraging interaction, collaboration, and feedback. Sellers can connect with customers through forums, social media

groups, and community events, building relationships and loyalty over time.

Popular Alternative Marketplaces

1. eBay: eBay is one of the world's largest online marketplaces, known for its auction-style listings, diverse product selection, and global reach. Founded in 1995, eBay allows sellers to list both new and used items for sale, set their own prices, and choose between auction-style or fixed-price listings. With millions of active users and listings across various categories, eBay offers sellers a platform to reach a broad and diverse audience of buyers.

2. Etsy: Etsy is a leading online marketplace for handmade, vintage, and artisanal goods, catering to a community of makers, creators, and craft enthusiasts. Founded in 2005, Etsy offers sellers a platform to showcase their unique and handmade products, connect with like-minded buyers, and build relationships with customers. With its focus on creativity, craftsmanship, and community, Etsy provides sellers with a supportive and vibrant marketplace to sell their products.

3. Bonanza: Bonanza is an online marketplace that prides itself on being a "seller-centric" platform, offering sellers low fees, flexible listing options, and a suite of tools to grow their businesses. With its focus on unique and one-of-a-kind items, Bonanza attracts buyers looking for personalized and hard-to-find products across various categories, including fashion, home decor, electronics, and collectibles.

4. Ruby Lane: Ruby Lane is an online marketplace specializing in vintage and antique goods, offering buyers a curated selection of high-quality and unique items from independent sellers and dealers. With its focus on authenticity, quality, and customer service, Ruby Lane provides sellers with a platform to showcase their vintage treasures and connect with discerning collectors and enthusiasts.

5. Poshmark: Poshmark is a social commerce platform that combines elements of social networking with e-commerce, allowing users to buy, sell, and discover fashion and accessories from their favorite brands and influencers. With its focus on community engagement, Poshmark offers sellers a platform to connect with fashion enthusiasts,

share their style inspiration, and monetize their closets.

Benefits of Selling on Alternative Marketplaces

1. Access to Niche Audiences: Alternative marketplaces allow sellers to reach niche audiences and target specific demographics, interests, and preferences. Whether it's vintage collectors on Ruby Lane or handmade enthusiasts on Etsy, alternative marketplaces offer sellers the opportunity to connect with engaged and passionate buyers in their respective niches.

2. Diversification of Sales Channels: Selling on alternative marketplaces enables sellers to diversify their sales channels and reduce reliance on any single platform or marketplace. By expanding their presence across multiple channels, sellers can mitigate risk, reach new customers, and maximize their revenue potential.

3. Lower Barrier to Entry: Alternative marketplaces often have lower barriers to entry compared to traditional retail channels, making it easier for independent sellers and small businesses to start selling online. With minimal upfront costs,

flexible listing options, and seller-friendly policies, alternative marketplaces provide a low-risk and accessible platform for aspiring entrepreneurs.

4. Supportive Community and Resources: Alternative marketplaces foster a supportive community of sellers, buyers, and enthusiasts, offering resources, tools, and guidance to help sellers succeed. From educational resources and seller forums to mentorship programs and networking events, alternative marketplaces provide sellers with the support and encouragement they need to grow their businesses.

5. Flexibility and Control: Alternative marketplaces offer sellers greater flexibility and control over their businesses, allowing them to set their own prices, manage inventory, and communicate directly with customers. With the ability to customize listings, track performance metrics, and iterate on strategies, sellers can adapt and evolve their businesses to meet changing market demands.

Best Practices for Selling on Alternative Marketplaces

1. Optimize Product Listings: Create detailed and compelling product listings that showcase your

products effectively and attract buyers' attention. Use high-quality images, descriptive titles, and detailed descriptions to highlight key features, benefits, and unique selling points.

2. Provide Excellent Customer Service: Prioritize excellent customer service to build trust, loyalty, and repeat business. Respond promptly to customer inquiries, address concerns and issues professionally, and strive to exceed customers' expectations at every touchpoint.

3. Leverage Social Media and Marketing: Leverage social media channels and marketing tactics to promote your products, engage with customers, and drive traffic to your listings. Use platforms like Instagram, Facebook, and Pinterest to showcase your products, share behind-the-scenes content, and connect with your audience.

4. Offer Competitive Pricing and Shipping: Price your products competitively and offer transparent shipping options to attract buyers and increase conversion rates. Consider offering free shipping, discounts, or promotions to incentivize purchases and drive sales.

5. Optimize for Search and Discovery: Optimize your product listings for search engines and marketplace algorithms to improve visibility and discoverability. Use relevant keywords, tags, and categories to help buyers find your products more easily and increase your chances of appearing in search results.

6. Build Trust and Credibility: Build trust and credibility with buyers by providing accurate product descriptions, transparent policies, and positive customer experiences. Encourage customer reviews and feedback, and showcase testimonials and endorsements to reassure buyers and build confidence in your brand.

Chapter 25

Customer Loyalty and Retention Strategies

In the fiercely competitive landscape of e-commerce, customer loyalty and retention are critical components of long-term success. While acquiring new customers is essential for growth, retaining existing customers and fostering strong relationships can drive sustainable revenue, repeat business, and brand advocacy. In this chapter, we'll explore the importance of customer loyalty and retention in e-commerce, uncover key strategies and tactics for building customer loyalty, and discuss best practices for retaining customers and maximizing lifetime value.

The Importance of Customer Loyalty and Retention

Customer loyalty and retention refer to the ability of a business to retain customers over time, cultivate strong relationships, and encourage repeat purchases. In the e-commerce context, customer loyalty is a key driver of business growth, profitability, and sustainability, as loyal customers tend to spend more, purchase more frequently, and act as brand advocates within their networks.

Key Benefits of Customer Loyalty and Retention

1. Increased Customer Lifetime Value (CLV): Loyal customers have a higher lifetime value compared to one-time purchasers, as they tend to make more purchases over time and contribute more revenue to the business. By focusing on customer retention and cultivating long-term relationships, businesses can maximize CLV and drive sustainable revenue growth.

2. Reduced Customer Acquisition Costs (CAC): Acquiring new customers can be costly and resource-intensive, requiring investments in marketing, advertising, and promotions. By retaining existing customers and encouraging repeat purchases, businesses can reduce CAC and improve overall marketing ROI, as loyal customers are more likely to purchase without the need for extensive marketing efforts.

3. Enhanced Brand Loyalty and Advocacy: Loyal customers are more likely to develop strong emotional connections with a brand and advocate for it within their social circles. By delivering exceptional customer experiences, providing personalized service, and fostering community engagement, businesses can turn satisfied customers into brand ambassadors who promote their products and services to others.

4. Competitive Advantage and Differentiation: In today's competitive marketplace, customer loyalty can serve as a powerful differentiator and competitive advantage. By delivering superior value, exceptional service, and memorable experiences, businesses can stand out from competitors and attract and retain loyal customers who choose their brand over others.

5. Improved Customer Satisfaction and Retention: Loyal customers are more satisfied with their overall shopping experience, more likely to recommend the brand to others, and less likely to switch to competitors. By prioritizing customer satisfaction, addressing customer needs and concerns, and delivering consistent value, businesses can foster loyalty and retain customers over the long term.

Key Strategies for Building Customer Loyalty and Retention

1. Deliver Exceptional Customer Experiences: Focus on delivering exceptional customer experiences at every touchpoint, from the moment customers visit your website to post-purchase support and service. Provide personalized recommendations, responsive customer service, and seamless interactions to delight customers and exceed their expectations.

2. Offer Loyalty Programs and Incentives: Implement loyalty programs and incentives to reward repeat purchases, encourage customer engagement, and foster loyalty. Offer perks such as discounts, rewards points, exclusive access, and special offers to incentivize customers to return and make additional purchases.

3. Personalize Communication and Marketing: Personalize communication and marketing efforts to cater to the individual preferences and needs of each customer. Use data and insights to segment customers based on behavior, purchase history, and demographics, and tailor messaging, offers, and recommendations accordingly.

4. Provide Proactive Customer Support: Provide proactive customer support and assistance to address customer inquiries, resolve issues, and ensure a positive shopping experience. Be responsive to customer feedback and complaints, and take proactive steps to resolve issues and prevent future problems.

5. Solicit and Act on Customer Feedback: Solicit feedback from customers through surveys, reviews, and feedback forms and use insights to improve products, services, and the overall shopping experience. Act on customer feedback promptly, address concerns and suggestions and demonstrate a commitment to continuous improvement.

6. Build Community and Engagement: Build a sense of community and engagement around your brand by fostering interaction, dialogue, and collaboration among customers. Create online forums, social media groups, and user-generated content platforms where customers can connect with each other, share experiences, and engage with your brand.

7. Focus on Product Quality and Innovation: Focus on product quality, innovation, and differentiation

to create compelling value propositions and drive customer loyalty. Continuously innovate and improve products based on customer feedback and market trends, and differentiate your brand through unique features, benefits, and value-added services.

8. Provide Value Beyond Transactions: Provide value beyond transactions by offering educational content, resources, and experiences that enrich customers' lives and align with their interests and aspirations. Become a trusted source of information and inspiration in your niche, and position your brand as a valuable partner in customers' journey.

Best Practices for Retaining Customers and Maximizing Lifetime Value

1. Segment Customers and Tailor Messaging: Segment customers based on behavior, preferences, and demographics and tailor messaging and offers to each segment. Use segmentation to deliver personalized communication, recommendations, and incentives that resonate with different customer groups.

2. Re-engage   Inactive   Customers: Re-engage inactive or dormant customers through targeted

reactivation campaigns, special offers, and personalized incentives. Use data and insights to identify customers who have lapsed in their purchasing activity and develop strategies to win them back.

3. **Offer Subscription and Recurring Revenue Models:** Offer subscription and recurring revenue models to encourage ongoing engagement and loyalty. Provide subscription-based products or services that offer convenience, value, and continuity and incentivize customers to subscribe with exclusive benefits and discounts.

4. **Implement Abandoned Cart Recovery Strategies:** Implement abandoned cart recovery strategies to recapture lost sales and convert abandoned shopping carts into completed purchases. Use automated email reminders, personalized offers, and retargeting ads to remind customers of their abandoned items and encourage them to complete their purchase.

5. **Provide Seamless Cross-Channel Experiences:** Provide seamless cross-channel experiences across multiple touchpoints and devices, allowing customers to engage with your brand wherever they are. Ensure consistency in messaging,

branding, and user experience across websites, mobile apps, social media, and offline channels.

6. Measure and Monitor Customer Retention Metrics: Measure and monitor key customer retention metrics such as customer churn rate, retention rate, and repeat purchase rate to track the effectiveness of your retention strategies. Use analytics and reporting tools to gain insights into customer behavior, identify trends, and optimize retention efforts.

7. Foster Customer Advocacy and Referrals: Foster customer advocacy and referrals by providing exceptional experiences and incentivizing customers to recommend your brand to others. Offer referral programs, discounts, or rewards for customers who refer friends and family, and leverage social proof and testimonials to showcase positive experiences.

8. Continuously Iterate and Improve: Continuously iterate and improve your customer retention strategies based on feedback, data, and insights. Test different approaches, measure results, and refine your tactics to optimize performance and drive long-term loyalty and retention.

Conclusion

In conclusion, customer loyalty and retention are essential components of long-term success in e-commerce, driving sustainable revenue, repeat business, and brand advocacy. By prioritizing customer satisfaction, delivering exceptional experiences, and fostering strong relationships, businesses can build loyalty, retain customers, and maximize lifetime value. Whether it's implementing loyalty programs, personalizing communication, or providing seamless cross-channel experiences, businesses can leverage a variety of strategies and tactics to cultivate loyalty and retain customers over the long term. By focusing on customer retention and building lasting relationships, businesses can create a loyal customer base that drives growth, fosters brand advocacy, and positions them for success in the competitive e-commerce landscape.

9 798894 466651